658.406 GRU ✓

BOOK NO: 301171

ITEM NO: 1962703

ALLT

D0620488

Implementing
Strategic
Change

A PRACTICAL GUIDE FOR BUSINESS

TONY GRUNDY

Implementing
Strategic
Change

A PRACTICAL GUIDE FOR BUSINESS

GWENT COLLEGE OF HIGHER EDUCATION

LIBRARY

ALLT-YR-YN LIBRARY

KOGAN
PAGE

Apart from any fair dealing for the purposes of research or private study, or criticism or review, as permitted under the Copyright, Designs and Patents Act, 1988, this publication may only be reproduced, stored or transmitted, in any form or by any means, with the prior permission in writing of the publishers, or in the case of reprographic reproduction in accordance with the terms of licences issued by the Copyright Licensing Agency. Enquiries concerning reproduction outside those terms should be sent to the publishers at the undermentioned address:

Kogan Page Limited
120 Pentonville Road
London N1 9JN
© Tony Grundy 1993

British Library Cataloguing in Publication Data

A CIP record for this book is available from the British Library.

ISBN 0 7494 0745 X

Typeset by DP Photosetting, Aylesbury, Bucks
Printed in England by Clays Ltd, St Ives plc

CONTENTS

PART THREE — ACCELERATING THE PROCESS

PART FOUR — STEERING STRATEGIC CHANGE

LIST OF FIGURES

9

PREFACE

This book began in response to the continued deputations from managers I receive when running in-company, strategic change programmes at a number of business schools. The busy manager in these companies is often bewildered by the sheer number of offerings on 'Managing Change', none of which seems to put the change process into a strategic context without becoming highly academic and theoretical. Senior managers have asked me on numerous occasions why someone has not written a practical guide to handling strategic change. So the basis for the book is demand coming directly from managers themselves. It is, therefore, written for them, and intended to be used on an everyday basis. It is not primarily targeted at the academic community, although it draws from the best models and tools of change management which theory tested out in practice can supply.

The need for a practical guide to enable managers to implement strategic change is, I believe, of pressing urgency. Despite the many management books on 'change' which have been written in the 1980s and early 1990s, few, if any, seem fully to address the need for a guide which is both relevant at the practical level, yet has theoretical foundation. Nor do most of the more readily accessible 'strategy' books help significantly with the issue of implementation, although this has been flagged up as important by some change 'gurus' in recent years.

The book contains several vivid cases of change in major organisations to illustrate the importance of understanding the context as well as the content of change. The case studies also highlight how to use 'the change tools' in practice. These change tools are further supported in Chapters 5 and 6 by a set of semi-structured questions as a prompt to thinking. Where appropriate, key terms are defined explicitly, so avoiding the excessive and unclear use of jargon common to so many management books.

The book is, therefore, a guide to implementing strategic change for both senior and middle managers. It will also be of interest for MBA courses which genuinely aim to create tomorrow's general manager, rather than to reinforce the (now old) joke that MBA simply means 'more boring analysis'. Indeed, the book does much to re-emphasise the importance of management process and practice alongside business analysis, which is traditionally at the core of most business school programmes.

Acknowledgements

I would like to thank Nicky Burton and Dave King (both formerly of Dowty), Kippa Alliston, Tom Boardman, Andrew Budge and Terry Youll of the Prudential and Trevor Mills and David Palk of ICL for their assistance in writing the core cases. In addition, I am indebted to Graeme Maxton of City University Business School and John Hendry of the Judge Institute of Management Studies, Cambridge University for their invaluable comments on the Blackbridge Technology Group case.

PART ONE

EXPLORING STRATEGIC CHANGE

1

INTRODUCTION

THREE STAGES OF IMPLEMENTING STRATEGIC CHANGE

Change management — a strategic process

'Managing Change' has become *the theme* for managers in the 1990s. Organisations have been struck externally by waves of rapid competitive change, by deregulation and re-regulation, by economic boom and recession, and through international turbulence. Internally, these shocks may have been amplified by quality programmes (sometimes pursued with a religious zeal) through corporate re-structuring (which often seems more like 'disorganisation' than 'reorganisation') and through the impact of office and communications technology.

This turbulence can be defined as follows:

> *Turbulence* is the apparently random and unpredictable way in which change occurs both externally and internally. (This apparent or real chaos is due to the often perverse interaction of internal and external change systems of the business and its environment.)

But even if we discount the hype that surrounds the change process, it is evident that managers now face a qualitatively different challenge to that faced in the 1970s and early 1980s. This is because the changes being managed now are not only more awe-inspiring and widespread, but also because managers are becoming more receptive to recognising change as a strategic process. Indeed, if we are concerned about managing strategic change in management, this would appear to require a strategic rather than a primarily tactical approach.

Despite the considerable amount of thinking which has gone on in strategic planning and in strategic management generally, few writers have sought to apply strategic thinking to practical issues in the management of change. Indeed, it has been said that 'Implementing Strategic Change' is regarded in many academic circles of strategic management as a 'mucky and murky area'. Yet, it is so often in the implementation of change that strategic planning traditionally runs to ground.

> *Strategic planning* can be defined as the creation of a sense of
> long-term direction in order to anticipate and shape the future
> environment, to allocate resources for competitive advantage
> and to steer change.

Where strategic thinkers have entered this territory they appear to be frightened of prescribing management approaches. This may be because one-time 'excellent' companies are now sinking into competitive distress and oblivion. It may also be because of a negative reaction to the plethora of 'how to survive' management books that clutter airport and high-street bookshops.

Yet, strategic thinking is surely an essential tool in helping implement strategic change. This book, or rather guide, contains in Part Two a tool-kit of techniques and processes through which complex and strategic change can be understood and mastered. These tools are supported by an extensive set of questions in the form of checklists which serve as prompts for creating strategic vision and for implementing necessary change.

These tools have been applied successfully (in different mixes) in a number of testing change environments (including the Dowty, Prudential and other cases) discussed here. This demonstrates that the process of strategic change is amenable to analysis through a combination of 'hard' and 'soft' tools. Strategic change is not just something which can be coped with by managers simply becoming 'more flexible and more adaptive', which encourages them to be more passive rather than less. It also requires rigorous thinking about issues, process and outcomes and a questioning attitude to both the status quo and to new areas of change.

Managers or masochists of change?

The core theme of this book is essentially a simple one. Managers are often reactive, submissive and sometimes sluggish when responding to strategic change. When there are additional deluges of change they react by working ever harder and faster to manage it more efficiently. This behaviour becomes surrounded by an air of 'we are having such a bad time in managing change and aren't we just so terribly busy coping with it'. Instead, much conventional thinking actually promotes the idea of 'change managers' — and of 'managing' change. This is *stage one* of implementing strategic change — where managers concentrate mainly on managing change more efficiently, but the change itself is considered as a given, possibly imposed from above.

Stage two of implementing strategic change occurs where managers also begin to address the issue of the effective management of change: they begin to review the processes of managing change to see if they can facilitate progress and remove blocks.

But there is a further phase — *stage three* — in the evolution of implementing strategic change. This arises when managers view change initiatives and activities, not in isolation, but in relation to the 'big picture' — in other words, at a strategic level. This may highlight gaps in programmes or existing processes for managing change, as well as raise questions about the strategic, operational, organisational and financial benefits that change aims to generate.

All too often, the 'benefits' of the change are assumed to have been well-evaluated, when these have only been broadly (and often vaguely) addressed by more senior management. Stage three thus involves proactive challenge upwards to the rationale of change, rather than taking change requirements as 'given'.

Moving into stage three mode requires a shift in organisational and individual style which some managers may find uncomfortable. But much of the continued pain experienced by companies when implementing strategic change comes from their being stuck in a mix of stages one and two which focus on efficiency and effectiveness only. Even where some managers have moved their mind-set into stages two and three to manage change strategically, they may feel hindered because of the reactionary attitudes of others.

It is now timely to introduce our first, main definition:

> *Strategic change* is the reshaping of strategy, structure and

culture of an organisation over time, by internal design, by external forces or by simple drift.

The above definition accommodates strategic change which is managed in a deliberate as opposed to an emergent or opportunistic way.

HOW THIS GUIDE WILL HELP YOU

This book contains not just a 'nice to have' set of tools but an essential guide for setting the overall direction for strategic change for a business, and for successful implementation of change projects to achieve these goals. These projects may be tangible and specific — for example, implementing systems or structure changes, or they may be less tangible and/or wide reaching, such as quality or culture change programmes. Change projects can be very large or equally very small.

The book seeks to achieve a number of key objectives:

- to demystify the issues of implementing strategic change (a task already begun in this chapter). For the reader who wishes to learn more about change theory, Appendix I will be additional, compulsory reading (especially for practically-orientated MBA students);
- to enable the rationale of a particular area of strategic change to be appraised (Chapter 2; and the checklists on strategic vision — Chapter 5);
- to provide a tool-kit for managing the change process and specific change issues at a micro-level (Chapters 3 and 4). This tool-kit, and the questionnaires in Chapters 5 and 6 of Part Two, give you an agenda for management of change, not merely in the short term. The hope is that you will continue to use these tools for the rest of your management career;
- to illustrate the use of these tools in three 'high intensity change' cases at Dowty, Prudential and at ICL, and in a case on 'strategic change in action' — Blackbridge Technology (Chapters 7-9 and Appendix II).

This book does not assume that putting change management into practice is a highly rational process. However, it proceeds on the basis that change issues which are less than clear can more effectively be managed by using some analysis tools, although many of these are 'soft' rather than 'hard' and precise.

Neither does the book assume that strategic change is always implemented through a planned process. Change is dependent upon context, and the style of implementation will vary, depending upon the degree of internal and external uncertainty and complexity.

To conclude this introduction, it may be useful for the reader to write down on one sheet of paper two lists, one for 'what key change problems does my organisation face?' and one for 'what key change issues do I face in my role?'. In each list you should identify *one* issue which you would like to resolve in parallel with reading this guide. If you can move a long way to resolving these two specific issues, then you will have taken the first step to incorporating these frameworks in your thinking and action.

The book also invites you to do a number of further exercises which will raise issues concerning the changes which you are facing. These provide immediate opportunities to use the change tools which will be introduced at each stage.

2

THE RATIONALE FOR CHANGE

INTRODUCTION

This chapter focuses on the underlying rationale behind any change process, beginning at the corporate or business level and then at the micro level to deal with issues faced by the individual manager. We begin by looking at the types of change, as these may vary. This leads on to exploring a framework for linking strategy, structure and culture. The three main levels of change are then distinguished: the 'macro' or business level, the 'micro' or change project level, and finally at the level of the individual. Although each of these levels is interrelated, it is useful to segregate them out as different factors which may come into play (see the section later on 'the many levels of change').

These frameworks are introduced purely to set the scene. This is analogous to planning a journey: first you begin with the country map, then with the region and then the local map. Indeed, understanding change is akin to using maps, but it requires some knowledge of what the symbols mean — the main routes, country roads, railways, hills, lakes, etc.

In the case of change we have, however, a mix of tangible and less tangible symbols — for example, structure, culture, quality and leadership. What must then occur — beginning in this chapter — is a process of unpicking how these may interrelate as we map our journey. We begin by looking at the varieties of change.

VARIETIES OF CHANGE

Many managers perceive 'change' as a homogeneous body and — to continue the metaphor of planning a journey — largely in an unmapped or partly mapped state. Other managers describe change as being primarily the enemy of stability. It is possible, however, to separate out a number of characteristic types of change. These 'varieties of change' are broad generalisations which can be used to help managers reflect on the relative severity of change which they face, rather than being empirically tested 'models'.

First, managers may experience smooth incremental change. This is a characteristic of business environments which have been evolving slowly and in a systematic and predictable way. Although few managers would characterise their change environment as having a 'smooth incremental' profile nowadays, this is likely to have been more prevalent in the predictably expanding markets of the 1950s, 1960s and through to the early 1970s. Nevertheless, even into the 1990s managers may believe (in exceptional cases) that a relatively smooth state of change is in place. Not all change contexts are turbulent or chaotic by any means.

Second, we may have a situation of 'bumpy incremental change'. This is characterised by periods of relative tranquillity punctuated by acceleration in the pace of change, which is then frequently perceived as 'overload'. These periods of overload are often associated with periodic reorganisation. Bumpy incremental change is, thus, akin to movement of continental land masses where the 'fault' enables periodic readjustment to occur without cataclysmic effect (although sometimes there might be an earthquake).

These triggers of change can be defined as follows:

> *Triggers of change* are the factors which may conspire to initiate change both internally and externally regardless of whether these are seen as needs, opportunities or threats.

The third variety of change is one of 'discontinuous change'. Although sometimes associated with 'bumpy incremental change' — where an external shock generates major change (for example in the UK brewing industry due to regulatory action in the late 1980s) — it is more typically associated with a break in the pattern of 'smooth incremental change'.

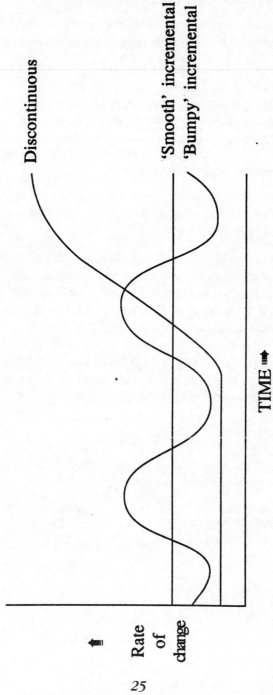

Figure 2.1 Major types of change

Discontinuous change can be defined as follows:

> *Discontinuous change* is change which is marked by rapid shifts in either strategy, structure or culture, or in all three.

To varying degrees, the cases in Chapters 5-7 all exhibit discontinuous change shaped by both external and internal forces.

This discontinuity can occur either because internal change has not kept up with external change, or where change in markets or regulation has propelled an organisation into a radically new way of operating. The privatisation of the electricity industry in the 1980s is a classic case of the latter, where rapid 'unfreezing' occurred:

> *Unfreezing* is the softening up of existing 'ways of doing things around here' and of underlying attitudes through a process of challenge and reflection.

One way of unfreezing managers' perceptions of their own change is to get them to sketch what they see as the pace of change going back in time. Using the characteristic curves of change (now illustrated in Figure 2.1), managers draw in their own impressions of change, pinpointing key surges in activity and also relating these back to stimulus events. The same principle can be used to project anticipated rates of change, given known (and assumed) events which are likely to trigger change. This is particularly stretching for all but the most visionary of management teams, but can be equally illuminating.

SHORT EXERCISE

Using Figure 2.1 as stimulus material, what kind of change do you face in your organisation? Does this most closely resemble:

- smooth incremental change?
- bumpy incremental change?
- discontinuous change?

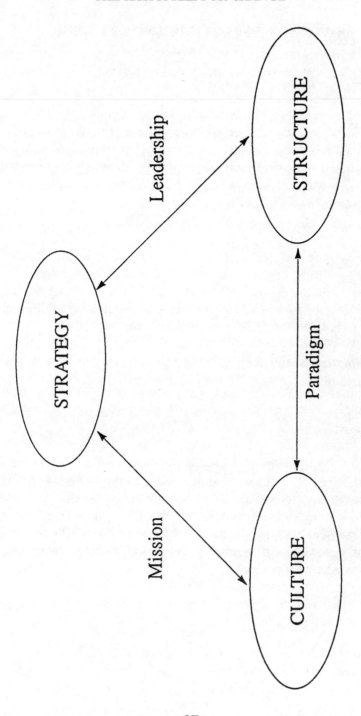

Figure 2.2 Managing strategic change

STRATEGY, STRUCTURE AND CULTURE — AND PARADIGMS

Capturing strategic change

Figure 2.2 now introduces us to a framework for understanding strategic change . Its origins lie in part with Peters and Waterman's (1982) 'Seven S's'. Recalling this framework, Figure 2.2 captures 'strategy' as a core part of the 'change system', staff, structure and 'hard' skills are subsumed under 'structure', whilst shared values, style and 'soft' skills are subsumed under 'culture' (see Appendix 1).

These three elements can be defined as follows:

> *Strategy* is the deliberate or emergent pattern of decisions which shape an organisation's future and its fit within its environment. These 'decisions' may involve changing the future scope and shape of activities or major areas of internal change aimed at protecting or enhancing capability.

> *Structure* is the formal reporting relationships, roles and clusters of activity within an organisation.

> *Culture* is the set of values, attitudes, beliefs and behaviours which are the unique hallmark of an organisation.

The idea underlying Figure 2.2 is that the three key elements of managing strategic change — strategy, structure and culture — need to be skilfully and consciously co-ordinated. (This is not to say that this is common in reality — in perhaps most cases, these three elements are seen as separate by management, without the need to be co-ordinated. The theme of the need for 'co-ordination' is recently taken up by interpretative theorists, Pettigrew and Whipp, 1991).

The core linkages between each of the three elements should now be examined in order to cement this need for co-ordination. For simplicity, these have been distilled into three key ingredients:

● between strategy and structure — *leadership*;
● between structure and culture — *the paradigm*;
● between culture and strategy — *mission*.

Providing inspiration and energy — leadership

The idea that leadership is a key link between strategy and structure comes from the observation that — because of a lack of appropriate leadership — having a clear 'strategy' may not necessarily produce effective implementation. Leadership plays a pivotal role in managing strategic change because without it 'the strategy' will not galvanise managers into appropriate action. However appropriate 'organisational structure' (or culture) is in fitting the strategy, it will not, of itself, prevent drift. Leadership is vitally important therefore, not merely as a part of the change management process (see Chapter 3) but also because of its symbolic role in reinforcing strategy and structure. It also plays an indirect but important role in shaping the 'paradigm' (see next section), or guidance system of an organisation.

Leadership can be defined as follows:

> *Leadership* is the living and symbolic embodiment of 'how we do things around here' — both now and in the future — whether this is as a leading team or as a single person.

'How we do things around here' — the paradigm

The link between structure and culture, or 'the paradigm', is of particular interest and may be novel to many managers. The 'paradigm' represents 'how we do things around here'. The origins of the 'paradigm' are to be found in the theory of science (Kuhn, 1962), but the idea has been popularised in the US by Barker and in the UK more recently at Cranfield (Johnson, 1992; Grundy and King, 1992). This 'paradigm' embraces a raft of organisational processes, some of which are 'hard' and tangible (the right-hand side of Figure 2.3) and some of which are 'soft' and intangible (the left-hand side of Figure 2.3) — for example, signals from key stakeholders.

The paradigm also comes from the idea of organisational culture, originally used by Marvin Bower, formerly managing director of McKinsey and Company, to capture the idea of 'how we do things around here'. However, the idea of 'how we do things around here' as the paradigm extends into more tangible structures and processes and beyond mere 'culture' — that is, if we understand culture as being the underlying values, attitudes, beliefs and behaviour within the organisation.

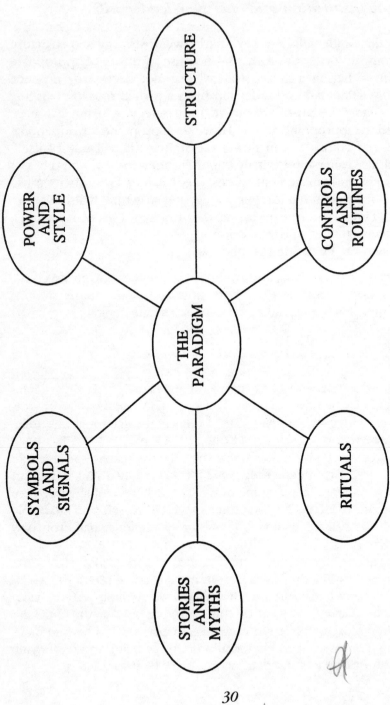

Note: This figure is a simplified version of Professor Johnson's 'culture web' (at Cranfield School of Management).

Figure 2.3 The paradigm

The 'paradigm' works almost like the equivalent of the 'unconscious mind' of the organisation, shaping how external change is interpreted, how strategic and tactical decisions are taken, and how internal change is managed. Newcomers to an organisation — including recruits, or for that matter consultants — will be a good deal more conscious of the peculiarity of 'the paradigm' than managers who have been with the organisation for many years.

The 'paradigm' influences strategic change in a variety of ways including:

- It filters events in the external environment and therefore channels how managers understand external change.
- It shapes the organisation's views on which newcomers it will 'bring aboard' — companies tend to recruit according to a view of fit with being 'one of us'.
- It plays an influential role in shaping the choice of leaders — except where that leader has been hired specifically to challenge or 'break' the paradigm.
- It also shapes in a profound way how strategic decisions are implemented and also how day-to-day operations are conducted.
- The paradigm may, therefore, work as a powerful inhibitor to change. Paradigm analysis is thus a powerful technique in bringing to the surface forces which impede or constrain change (see Chapter 4 on Change Tools).

Daring to analyse the paradigm

The 'paradigm' is often intermingled with competing patterns of 'how we do things around here'. For example, in Chapter 7 on strategy-led change at Dowty Communications, on the one hand controls were being tightened, but on the other there was an opposing desire to be 'more entrepreneurial'. (Opposing paradigms can even be found within the same person's behaviour at different times — it does not have to be discovered in competing factions.) In the Dowty case, tightening up structural influences (the right-hand side of 'the paradigm') produced a tendency to 'crowd out' the softer entrepreneurial influences (culture) which had governed the organisation previously. This tension may conspire to turn 'the paradigm' into, in effect, a 'paradox' or perhaps in its worst case, 'paralysis'.

Paradigm analysis may also produce competing views of 'how we do things around here', highlighting confusion in the organisation. This may reveal the existence of both sub-cultures and sub-structures within different functions or decisions. These may fragment the organisational unconscious (as in Johnson's 1992 example of a major UK consulting firm).

This argument raises the issue as to what extent diversity of paradigm should be managed or tolerated. It may be impossible to bring a divergent sub-paradigm into line where there are strong reinforcing factors, unless these themselves are attacked. For instance, if a sales force has a strong sub-paradigm it may be necessary to adjust core rewards and recognition systems. But changes in the rewards and recognition systems of the sales force may be limited by both operational and financial constraints. For instance, the sales force's sub-paradigm may reflect specific routines which have proved workable in dealing with target customers. Sales people may thus be unable to 'toe the line' and reflect the core paradigm of the company.

The 'paradigm' can be used to plot the overall path of strategic change, particularly to diagnose:

- ' where we are now;'
- ' where we want to be.'

This can be done either using the parts of the paradigm to perform specific analyses for each one of its key ingredients — for example 'power', 'structure', 'routines', 'stories', 'symbols', etc. Or the paradigm 'ingredients' can be used as a check-list to stimulate reflection on 'how we do things around here' as opposed to 'how we might like to do them'.

SUGGESTED EXERCISE

Using the paradigm tool as a stimulus for ideas, write down four key aspects of 'how we do things around here now' versus how you would like to see this changing in the future. To focus this analysis it may be worthwhile selecting from the current paradigm four areas which are *not* conducive to performance and picturing how each of these may be radically improved in the future.

The paradigm can also be used to analyse progress of change mid-way through. This can be done by comparing the current position against that at the very beginning of your current change process. For each key element of the paradigm which you wish to focus in on, ask:

> Where are we now (compared with where we were), as opposed to where we need to be?

Managers within Prudential Life Administration (Chapter 8) successfully experimented with this approach. About eighteen months into a major change process they scored each dimension of the paradigm on a scale of 1-5 (1 being their starting point, 5 being the 'paradigm ideal'). This produced some revealing insights into the scale of the change gap which still remained.

Don't dabble in paradigm change

The virtue of the 'paradigm' lies both in its relative simplicity and in its ability to embrace a web of key factors in the strategic change process. It is also powerful in bringing to the surface issues of a less tangible nature which are typically overlooked by managers. Although some management thinkers claim to take the credit for discovering this trophy, the fundamental idea dates back to changing paradigms in scientific discovery (Kuhn, 1962). It is useful to remember these origins — just as in science we find theoretical paradigms to be sticky and resistant to change, so the old paradigm in an organisation may fight back when it is threatened. This also implies that more successful changes (or perhaps more accurately 'shifts') in paradigm are accomplished by displaying more fundamental change as being consistent with 'how we do things around here' — or at least with the idealised paradigm of 'how we *should* do things around here'.

Paradigm-breaking as a head-on change strategy is a difficult exercise. Although there may be instances where this is essential, an attempt to mobilise change based purely on a confrontational strategy rarely proves workable. This requires wholesale dismantling of existing structures through powerful leadership. This may be a costly exercise where existing structures, although complex, add value to customers and channels to market rather than dissipate value. But in other instances, paradigm breaking may be vital for competitive survival. Paradigm breaking is thus best defined as:

> *Paradigm breaking* is a deliberate attempt to produce a radical and revolutionary change in 'how we do things around here'.

In most instances, it is more feasible to attempt a more modest paradigm shift which can be defined as:

> A *paradigm shift* is a concerted attempt to move the paradigm from one state to another whilst retaining some, but not all, of its core features.

We have devoted a lot of space to paradigms and justly so, because they prove useful in interpreting change throughout the rest of this book. But it is now opportune to turn to the ingredient of 'mission' which, it is argued, can form a key link between culture and strategy.

Is it a 'mission' or just a mirage?

Many European companies appear to be ambivalent about the concept of 'mission'. They divide approximately into three camps: those who dislike the idea of 'mission' because of US connotations; those who are ambivalent and may want a 'mission' (feeling that without it they are not somehow fully clothed) but being unsure what they might do with it once they have got it; finally, there are those who have it and (usually) it has acquired an aura like the celebrated biblical tablets of stone. Rarely do we see 'mission' genuinely being used to guide action and behaviour, whether strategic or tactical. But without it, there is a major danger that 'strategy' becomes unhooked from the softer and crucial ingredients of culture in the strategic change process.

'Mission' is a word much misused in management circles. It can be perhaps best defined as:

> *Mission* is the purpose, aims and values of an organisation which help define the intended scope of the business and the anticipated rewards to stakeholders.

The above definition contains a number of elements which, at first sight, seem dissimilar. The purpose, aims and values of an organisation act as the internal guidance system, whilst the other elements — scope and stakeholder rewards — give a more tangible handle against which the 'mission's' fulfilment can be tested.

The mission can be used to steer strategy and also as a check on whether the strategy fulfils stakeholder needs and fits the values of the organisation. However, this does not always work well. The worst excesses of 'mission' may occur when this is derived as part of a change

34

process driven by an ambitious, but perhaps unrealistic, strategy for growth. A typical scenario runs like this: a company is seeking to fulfil the (high) expectations of both its shareholders and employees and seeks to expand by (either or both) organic and acquisitive growth of X per cent per annum.

Like the first cars, where a man used to go ahead on the road with a light, a mission is created to enable the organisation to reach out into the future, probing at or beyond the time horizon of its current strategy. This typically culminates in what might be termed a 'strategic wish list' which often contains such statements as 'to double in size in three (or five) years' or 'to become an international company in XYZ markets'. Mission statements of this kind are better called 'mirage statements' as they can do a lot more harm than good and misguide managers. Typically, they do not articulate how growth is to be attained (and also profitably) through developing competitive position. Also, it is not uncommon to find the 'mission' to be well beyond existing organisational and operational capability.

Having now put a firm 'health warning' on mission statements, they can nevertheless play a powerful role in sending a simple and coherent message throughout the organisation. This can spell out, not merely the broad strategic direction, but also how the organisation will move itself forward. But they may also unwittingly add to a sense of rigidity which may impede rather than facilitate a more flexible process of change and adaptation. Finally, they may require more effort to sustain than most managers are prepared ultimately to put in.

Despite recent emphasis on 'mission' (for example, Campbell and Tawadey, 1990) there appear some real doubts about over-selling the idea of formal 'mission' in practice. It does have an important part to play in driving strategic change, particularly in linking strategy and culture. However, it needs not only to be more carefully thought through in content terms (what it says), but also in how it is presented and used by management. The ideal 'mission' is something which is not pure motherhood, but is distinctive to the organisation. It should also reflect its internal and external context, at a given point. Yet, it needs to have flexibility to ride out tactical changes in the business.

SHORT EXERCISE

Do you have a clear 'mission' — either formally or informally within your organisation? Do you think it is complete and coherent? Is it more likely to guide or misguide management?

THE MANY LEVELS OF CHANGE

The different animals of change

So far, we have dealt with higher-level changes at the organisational unit level, whether this is the business or the corporate entity. It is often helpful to think of these as 'macro-level' changes. This is in contrast to the implementation of change at a more localised level, which it is useful to think of as being the 'micro level'. For example, the implementation of a new information system can be typically viewed as an important but 'micro-level' change. Alternatively, a specific change in working practices to implement a quality management is a macro change issue (as it impacts directly on the paradigm).

> *Macro* level change is thus any change with significant impact
> on strategy, structure or culture across the organisation. *Micro*
> level change is any change with more narrow or local impact.

In addition to macro and micro levels of change, there is also the issue of change at the level of the individual . This may cover a range of areas, including managing the effects of change to an existing role, taking on a new role, or even changing the style with which the role is executed. Strategies for individual change can be evolved just as much as they can for the macro and micro levels. In the course of analysis some interesting parallels can be observed — for example, between the macro-level paradigm of 'how we do things around here' versus the individual level 'how I do things around here'.

The theme of 'unfreezing'

Whether change is at a macro, micro or individual level, it typically involves an unfreezing process followed by a re-freezing process as the change is consolidated and stabilised. Unfreezing can be achieved either through forcing the change through (in which case resistances are stirred up) or by a more gentle and effective thawing out process by introducing an awareness of the need to change gradually.

One approach to the thawing out of an existing paradigm is to induce managers to reflect on their change issues. As part of a deliberate 'unfreezing programme', it is possible to get managers to reflect on all three 'levels of change' — macro, micro and individual. For instance, on change programmes at one leading business school all three levels are covered within the same workshop. This might begin with issues of either an individual or micro-level nature ('Reflect on a past change you have been involved in'). This might move on to consider change themes and forces driving change within the organisation as a whole, before then focusing on some more specific, micro-level business issues. Typically, these are areas of change which managers are responsible for driving forward themselves, either individually or as teams. Finally, the individual develops change action plans. These embrace issues which he or she faces over the following twelve months. In addition, these plans can cover personal changes in style, skills and career strategy of a longer-term nature.

Analysis at these three levels often builds up powerful learning momentum. This is steadily reinforced by repeated use of change tools, and by uncovering similar change structures and processes at the three different levels. In one case, a manager at a trading conglomerate evaluated (following a business school workshop) a major area of business change. Not only did he apply the 'change tools' which we will see in Chapters 3 and 4, but he did so with a flair and directness which left board members who witnessed his presentation stunned, yet not in defensive mode (especially as he had carefully worked through an analysis of key stakeholders, and developed influencing strategies which shaped the presentation).

SHORT CASE EXAMPLE

A senior manager from a financial services company attended a two-day workshop on managing change which focused on four key change issues within the business. He was exposed to a variety of change tools, including the paradigm, force-field analysis and stakeholder analysis. After the workshop, he began to experiment using these tools on a raft of issues on

---

a day-to-day basis. Initially, his team thought that this would rapidly wear off — akin to the effect of losing sun-tan after a Mediterranean holiday.

Instead of the effects wearing off, his change tools became firmly incorporated into his management routines. Two years later, his office could be found not as a stark, bureaucratic coffin, but as a room whose walls were peppered with change issues — analysed using the same tools: paradigm, force field and stakeholders.

Following this introduction, it is now time to move on to the impact of variations in the context of change.

MANAGING THE CHANGE CONTEXT

Beware fixed recipes for change

Many managers seek (but do not find) ready-made answers to what they perceive as being intractable change problems. But the context of change varies enormously, making it impossible to resolve change problems according to a fixed and mechanistic set of rules. 'Context' is one of the three key dimensions of 'change' which is highlighted by Pettigrew and Whipp (1991), the full triad being — content, context and process. We deal with process in Chapter 3 and tools for analysing content in Chapter 4. But it is context which makes it impossible to apply a fixed set of recipes for implementing strategic change across organisations, or even within the same organisation as history unfolds.

Importing change

Context is manifold. First, context includes the external environment within which the business or group is operating. This may include not merely changes within the industry structure (Porter, 1985), but also in the political, economic, social and technological environment (or 'PEST' factors). In the main, managers are able to get to grips relatively quickly with issues relating to the external environment. What may prove more difficult is gaining a genuine understanding of the dynamics of change within the organisation, which may act over a long period. The important factors here are not merely 'events' (of the kind that you will read in a 'company history') but also less tangible shifts in leadership, management style and culture. Organisational change does not happen in a vacuum, but forms part of a web of historical development. Where this history is not fully appreciated, attempts to intervene to reshape the progress of change can become extremely difficult to take forward. This is a particular danger, for example, where a new chief executive is appointed from outside and brings his own recipes for change and his 'paradigm' from a company with different external context and paradigm.

SHORT CASE EXAMPLE

The chief executive of a major blue chip company was headhunted to become chairman of a large service organisation. This company was in need of turnaround as a result of inadequate financial performance and threatened deregulation of its markets and competitive entry. Although he succeeded in making some early and incisive changes in the company's structure and in strategy, by the time he had been in position for 18 months the strain of working within an entirely different culture (and one which proved extremely resilient to his intervention) began to take its toll. He found it increasingly difficult to sustain his earlier incisive impact on management and had to look to new forms of leveraging the intervention.

The above example highlights not only the resistances encountered when a major culture change is required, but also how this may place taxing demands on the leader. However charismatic and charged with energy, it is easy to underestimate the time-scale required to effect major culture change, and to dissipate much energy within the first six to nine months of the intervention.

From past experience, managers rarely appear to reflect explicitly on past changes with which they or their organisations have been involved — so often, an understanding of historical (and also the cultural) context is lacking. Managers seem to find it impossible to prevent themselves from 'plunging in' to 'get the job done', rather than spend time reflecting on the context for change.

Exploiting capability

The final element of 'change context' which needs to be highlighted is 'organisational capability'. Again, this is often taken for granted, not only in terms of operational or competitive capability but also in terms of specific capability in managing change. In a change workshop where managers are questioned about whether a number of organisations are in general 'good' or 'not so good' at managing change, a typical response is: 'Oh yes, we are all used to change'. Managers mistake being buffeted by change with managing it effectively. In a masochistic way, they are 'used to it' without necessarily being competent at managing it.

Organisational capability is a large subject in its own right and warrants as much in-depth analysis as competitive analysis (which is more outward facing) in developing business performance. This is highlighted graphically by both Pettigrew and Whipp's exhaustive analysis (1991) and also in Ulrich and Lake's excellent diagnostic book (1990) on capability. We return to the issue of capability in more depth in Chapter 3 on change process.

KNOWING 'WHY' — THE RATIONALE FOR CHANGE

The flavour of the month syndrome

This final section brings together many of the earlier ideas of Chapters 1 and 2. In Chapter 1 it was highlighted that managers see the initially perceived 'change issue' revolving principally around managing change more efficiently. So often, the basic rationale for change is not examined, or, if it is, this is done cursorily.

A classic example of this is when quality initiatives are introduced within organisations. Often, this is done as a tactical response to perceived operational difficulties, or perhaps purely or primarily as a response to regulatory pressure (for instance, to comply with British Standard 5750). Worse still, it is introduced as a 'management fad' because 'other leading companies are doing it' — the copycat syndrome.

Where change initiatives such as quality are ill-thought through in terms of rationale (strategically, operationally, organisationally and financially), this is likely to infect the entire implementation process. Worse still, the predictable (and early) waves of cynicism which are generated undermine not only senior management's credibility, but indeed other efforts to integrate the strategic change process.

Did we forget to define the problem?

The problem of establishing a clear rationale for any change is an example of the wider but age-old difficulty of 'defining the problem' (or opportunity). Managers are often unable or unwilling to more than skim the surface of a problem, with the inevitable result that they see just symptoms, not the underlying problem. This is probably more to do with the management race to achieve results, rather than because managers are inherently stupid or incompetent. The race to achieve results, together with a fragmentation of activity, allows managers little time for reflection: their 'thinking windows' on change are usually too narrow to analyse difficult change issues unless aided by tools and processes which can temporarily lift them out of this rush.

To illustrate these problems, a head of manpower development for a UK bank recently pointed out:

> I do get cross when managers go on and on about 'their problems' when what they are actually talking about is possible solutions. For instance, you hear them complain that they have not had enough space in our administrative centre. But why is this such a 'problem' after all? They don't seem to have realised that their real problem is they don't need all those files, all that paper anyway, but haven't worked out a way of coping without it all.

The above example described problem-definition at an operational level. But these difficulties are also characteristic of the strategic level. For instance, Senge (1990) points out that when a strategy doesn't seem to be working, managers switch from strategy to strategy, furiously trying to find one which appears to work. But what is especially interesting, according to Senge (1990), is that when managers switch from strategy to strategy, rarely do they stand back and reflect why the strategy is not working.

Managing the boredom threshold

Senge's problems with strategy are mirrored in the change process. Where 'the business' does not seem to be performing up to its expectations, managers shift gear quickly (sometimes crunching them) and initiate new change. Sometimes, this crystallises in attempts to improve the organisation's strategic posture. More frequently, re-organisation, re-structuring and cost-cutting are triggered, involving major operational and organisational change. It may be, however, that the fundamental cause of strategic (and financial) decline has been missed. Also, the change measures may, far from improving the situation, aggravate the problem through putting an increasing burden on the organisation. This burden can also feed through to a longer-term loss of capability through a cycle of overload followed by declining morale.

Many managers do not seem to be aware of the cost of ill-focused change. It is pertinent to ask: was some (broad-brush) estimation of the financial cost/benefits of a re-organisation really thought through? Did this include indirect benefits and costs? In short, was there a business case put forward for the change? Did this identify how intangible benefits would be targeted and subsequently measured? (For a more detailed discussion of this topic, see Grundy (1992) *Corporate Strategy and Financial Decisions* .)

How to get your head clear

This line of argument now helps us to distil ten key questions which, if boldly addressed, may help clarify the rationale of any major change in the following short exercise:

SHORT EXERCISE

For a major change you are currently managing:

- How does the proposed change improve the external, strategic posture of the organisation?
- What effect will it have on internal, organisational capability — both short-term and long-term?
- What will it cost us — both directly and indirectly?
- What are the targeted financial and non-financial benefits and when will we expect to see them and with what degree of certainty?
- Does this particular change link with other areas of change so that it becomes part of a 'change convoy'?
- Given the other demands on managers, and the level of commitment to the change, does the proposed change appear feasible?
- If the change appears impossible how can it be simplified or re-formulated so that it becomes manageable?
- Will events (either external or internal) move so fast that the change rationale may rapidly become overtaken?

- What other options will implementing this particular change strategy foreclose for us?
- Can we define the rationale for the change in one short, sharp sentence which is readily communicable?

The rationale for change should thus be absolutely explicit about how it relates to the strategic, operational, financial and organisational objectives for the business. It must also identify its relationship with the organisational paradigm (structure linked in with culture). It needs to be set against both a historical context and that of the external environment. Finally, it needs to be linked with other areas of change to assess its potential to disrupt operational continuity, and to evaluate both the costs and risks of change.

Being clear about the rationale for change is only a necessary (but not a sufficient) condition of implementing strategic change effectively. In order to secure all the conditions required for success, there is equal need for managing the change process effectively, which we turn to next.

3

MANAGING THE CHANGE PROCESS

This chapter explores the important elements of the change process in depth. Many of these elements may appear to be self-evident once we have related them to practical examples of change. However, these are likely to be more novel to many managers who have not previously had the time or opportunity to reflect about the change process. Let us begin by defining the change process as follows:

> The *change process* is the process of diagnosing, planning, implementing, controlling and learning from change.

In order to explore the change process we need to focus therefore on a number of areas including:

- managing the dynamics of change;
- leadership and the stages of change;
- how major changes are triggered;
- staging deliberate interventions.
- people and capability;
- managing expectations and communication.

MANAGING THE DYNAMICS OF CHANGE

Much of the credit for highlighting the dynamic effects of change process lies with Carnall (1986). Carnall highlights that change typically goes through a series of stages — denial, defence, discarding, adapting, internalising. These stages are characterised as follows:

- Denial — during which there is typically paralysis, confusion, feelings of being overwhelmed, and performance begins to dip. During this phase new ideas or proposed changes are often rejected due to lack of fit with the organisational paradigm — often on spurious grounds.
- Defence — this is often manifested in depression and frustration, territorial fighting, ritual behaviour, and performance sags. These resistances occur due to territorial protection or through instinctive defences from existing culture or structure (the paradigm).
- Discarding — in this phase optimism emerges, and there is questioning commitment to the new 'trial' behaviour. During this phase old ways of 'how we do things around here' are given up.
- Adapting — during this phase a good deal of learning occurs, there are setbacks, there is re-trial but frustration may still occur, and performance begins to recover. During this phase the change strategy may need to be re-shaped to be fully assimilated.
- Internalising — finally within this phase new behaviours are accepted, self-esteem is re-built, and performance recovers. Here, new 'ways of doing things around here' are incorporated into the existing paradigm or within a new paradigm.

The above cycle is very similar to Lewin's (1935) earlier ideas of 'unfreezing' as a stage prior to implementing the change followed by 'refreezing' after the change as a bedding down process of routinisation and diffusion.

This cycle can span a considerable time, depending on how fundamental and challenging the change is and also to what extent the organisation, team or individual is adaptable. However, Carnall's theory is of great practical importance as it emphasises that there is invariably some decline in performance associated with a major change.

This decline in performance puts managers in a double bind. In many instances, the change itself has been initiated in order to improve performance. Yet the very impact of change acts to weaken performance. As change progresses, senior managers see a gap between actual and expected performance opening up, and they may push ever harder on the more tangible change levers. This response may provoke an even sharper drop in performance than would otherwise have occurred. Thus a vicious

46

cycle is put in motion, making the 'performance gap' assume chasm-like proportions.

While this is going on, the 'self-esteem' or morale of the organisation generally begins to do some peculiar things, according to Carnall. First, there may be some excitement and sense of uplift as a wave of change is about to crystallise. At last (managers think), something is going to be done about a problem or to resolve a nagging uncertainty. But as the change unfolds this typically amplifies uncertainty which deflates self-esteem at the organisational, team and individual level. This may lead to a collapse in morale.

This collapse in morale is usually triggered by the behaviour of senior management which conspires to aggravate uncertainty and increase stress. Frightened of spelling out the nature and implications of the change, senior managers seek to hold these implications close to their chests. Few organisations find it possible to prevent the nature and meaning of change from being transparent at a relatively early stage, except where managers adopt an ostrich-like approach. The dip in self-esteem (and also in performance) which results is a direct response to poor communication by senior management.

CASE EXERCISE

Identify one major change that you have been involved in personally in the past (either as initiator or on the receiving end). How did the self-esteem of those involved in the change behave before, during and after the change was initiated? How did the change affect the performance of those people which it impacted upon, again both, before, during and after? How did shifts in self-esteem and performance interact with one another over time — either positively or negatively?

Going back now to the premise therefore that all major change is accompanied by some degree of performance dip (relative to what would have occurred otherwise — at least in the short term), let us now examine alternative change scenarios.

In Figure 3.1 a change curve is depicted in Scenario 1 plotting self-esteem and performance over time which has a Carnall-like shape. This might have been generated, for instance, by a hypothetical re-structuring exercise. Note the slight decline in performance before the change begins, followed by a swift fall in performance. This fall is due to the

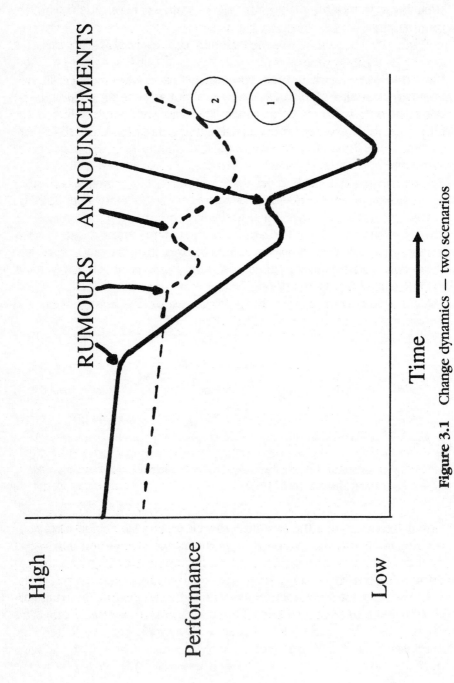

Figure 3.1 Change dynamics — two scenarios

implications of pending change being muffled through inadequate communication. Also, the 'change message' is left open-ended as 'we need to re-structure now and we may still need to take further steps to improve our competitiveness'.

By contrast, Scenario 2 is a hypothetical case where managers have been more explicit to key stakeholders about the scope of change, its rationale and also in its boundaries. This was well-communicated to gatherings of all personnel. Note that the change is announced at more or less the same time that 'rumours' began, minimising the degree of concern that mounted in Scenario 1. Although there is still some dip in performance, its severity is a lot less pronounced than that of Scenario 1. But perhaps more importantly, performance then reaches a level *beyond* its previous peak as overall capability has been enhanced.

For any change it is possible to sketch a curve of self-esteem and performance both before the change is implemented and also after the event. This is useful in anticipating the disruption effects of change and also in learning from change in action.

The lessons from this analysis of the dynamics of change are that:

- Performance is adversely affected by change and sometimes in a profound way.
- The 'dip' in performance can vary enormously depending on factors such as the quality of communication and leadership.
- It also varies depending on how flexible and responsive to change the organisation is, and its capability and capacity to manage the change process effectively.
- The factors which drag down performance may persist for a considerable period as the organisation adjusts unevenly to a new way of doing things (thus linking in with the idea of the 'paradigm').

In conclusion, visualising the dynamics of change provides a means of thinking through the inter-dependencies between the effective planning and implementation of change, the context of the change and finally the resulting impact on performance. It also highlights that implementing a major change is costly — at least in the short and medium term. This illustrates once more the need to be absolutely clear about the rationale for change and for this rationale to be supported by clearly targeted benefits.

LEADERSHIP AND THE STAGES OF CHANGE

The next important contribution to our understanding of the change process is the five-stage model. This links directly to the earlier definition of the change process at the beginning of this chapter. The model defines the following stages of change:

- diagnosis;
- planning;
- implementation;
- control;
- learning.

These five stages are also supported by the key co-ordinating mechanism of leadership. The virtue of this model lies in its simplicity and applicability to any change process, whether this is at macro, micro or the individual level (see Figure 3.2).

Any change might go through five stages of the model — but this is not to say that they always do. Managers may leap from a cursory diagnosis through to rudimentary planning and directly into the action or implementation mode. There may be some attempt to control this change but probably very little time spent on deliberately reflecting on or learning from the change. Thus, in practice, the 'five stage' model may be manifest only in a patchy form.

In order to make absolutely clear what each stage refers to, consider the following definitions:

Diagnosis is the process of understanding the rationale (that is why we are doing it) and implications of the change. Effective diagnosis involves exploring the forces which may enable or constrain the process of achieving the change objective (that is, what we want out of it). This may also involve exploring the stakeholders in the change and the impact of the change on the organisational paradigm.

Planning is the programming of one or more change thrusts or projects to mobilise resources, co-ordinate activities and to achieve desired milestones and outputs.

Implementation is the execution of change programmes and the management of barriers to change.

Control is the checking back to ensure that the change process is on track in terms of its benefits and costs (both expected and unexpected), and timescales.

Learning is the systematic review of lessons gained from the change, both in terms of the change rationale and also of the effectiveness of the change process. (This does not mean there is no learning in earlier stages, simply that a more formal, learning review is appropriate.)

When managers are asked to use the five-stage model to diagnose a) a 'successful' change which they have been involved in in the past, and b) a 'less successful' change, the model may reveal some important insights. Typically, those changes which were considered to be 'more successful' were ones where significant time and effort was spent on the more 'peripheral' stages of diagnosis, planning and learning. Conversely, less successful changes were typically 'implementation' only orientated. In one group of managers (an extreme example) it appeared that they had not even thought about stages other than implementation — far from appearing simple, this model appeared to be of an order quite different from their previous mind-set.

Another useful approach to teasing out how most managers actually manage the change process, is to ask them to estimate how much of the total time which they spend in the change process is spent on each stage. They are then asked how much they should spend on each stage. (This can be focused on a specific area of change if this is helpful.) Typical subjective estimates of effort and time expended run like this:

	Time actually spent	Time which should be spent
Diagnosis	2%	20%
Planning	10%	20%
Implementation	80%	40%
Control	6%	10%
Learning	2%	10%

Note the enormous difference in time between what, in an ideal world, it is felt that managers should spend on 'diagnosis' and what they actually spend.

CASE EXERCISE

For a change which you are about to embark upon, draw up a profile of how much time and effort you will devote to each one of the change phases. How does this compare with either a) the implicit plans you had, prior to this exercise, or b) how the balance of efforts previously on similar types of change projects?

The above model provides a continual reminder of how best to allocate effort during the change process. It helps ensure that managers can switch over from focusing primarily on efficient change management to effective change management. Indeed, in many cases the 'diagnosis' phase reveals that 'the problem' has been misidentified, enabling managers to move away from a mistaken change strategy.

The model itself comes from a composite number of sources. The underlying thinking comes from the project management literature which emphasises great care in defining the project and the separation of the more detailed project planning phase from definition. It also emphasises the value of a discrete 'learning' phase following the project, in sympathy with seeing change as an 'open learning process' (Senge, 1990) illustrated in the following example:

EXAMPLE — CHANGE AS A LEARNING PROCESS

A trading company recently piloted a quality programme. This was used to transform one of its UK sites from being an operation with internal inefficiency and the external impression of being 'scruffy and disorderly' to one which was customer friendly, orderly and efficient. Although the site benefited considerably from the impact of quality management, the main benefits of this successful exercise were found in the learning lessons gained throughout the business prior to a roll-out to the rest of the organisation.

Moving back again to the five-stage model, Figure 3.2 also highlights that the various stages are iterative. An important point to remember is that during detailed planning, and indeed even in implementation, the change team may need to revisit the 'diagnosis' phase. In several well-known companies where change projects were being managed by multi-

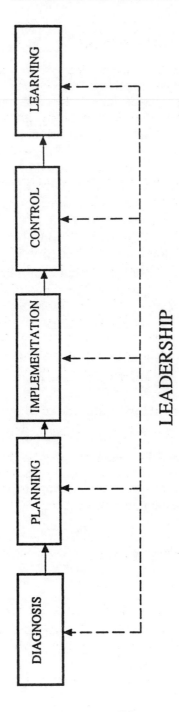

Figure 3.2 Key elements in managing change successfully

functional teams, team members were taken aback when the rationale of their project twisted and turned unpredictably, as it were, in mid-flight. This can be normal and essential as the nature of the objectives of change become refocused on the underlying problem as more data is gathered and assimilated. However, it re-emphasises the need to be as clear as possible about the objectives of the project in diagnosis phase, before beginning detailed planning, especially to minimise undesired and unintended effects.

Finally, support for change needs to be provided by means of effective leadership. This is an essential 'soft' force to what is otherwise a 'hard' model. Leadership is essential to guide any change through the five-stage process. For instance, senior management should be involved substantially in the diagnosis and learning phases and also where there is iteration between phases. This does not necessarily have to be leadership through autocratic style (whether benevolent or not) but may well be through orchestrating or facilitating change. This 'leadership' may be shared between the formal leader and other change agents or catalysts as we will see in the later section on 'interventions'.

TRIGGERS OF MAJOR CHANGE

Major changes can be triggered by a multitude of factors, particularly:

- External: changes in competitive forces, ~~regulation or~~ deregulation, changes in customer expectations and shifts in standards, and technology change occur.
- Internal: performance dips, ~~or change occurs in the~~ management team (particularly the chief executive).

Major change often crystallises when a number of factors converge. For instance, external competitive pressures may have intensified at the same time that internal performance appears flagging. An incoming chief executive also wants to make his or her mark on the organisation. Where these influences coincide this can produce a 'wave of change' which managers find it difficult to cope with.

Equally, where top management has been in place for some time, it is hard to put major change into effect. Lack of movement in top people appears to have the insidious effect of making the organisation brittle: if major change is instigated it either refuses to budge or alternatively, it breaks. A leader in this position may often espouse the need for change but in practice, be unwilling to take the first steps to implementing it because of fear about his/her personal position. This is aggravated if the change upsets what would otherwise be a fairly stable (internal) situation.

CASE EXERCISE

For a major change that you have thought about initiating in the past, what were your feelings and thoughts as you contemplated pushing your finger on the 'go button'? Were these thoughts and feelings influenced a) significantly, b) moderately, or c) not at all by the possible impact on your position in the organisation or your (personal) ambitions? Are there lessons for how you separate out business, political, and your personal objectives for the future?

STAGING DELIBERATE INTERVENTIONS

Bringing together the key players

This next section takes us a step back from the change process. It focuses especially on the role of key players within a major change and how this may change over time.

Interventions in organisations often involve a number of disparate elements. At the very early stages key players may use a change catalyst — usually the chief executive — who drives the change and who plays a major role early on in launching the change. Frequently, the chief executive plays a leading role in positioning the need for 'culture change' by personal involvement in culture change activities.

> The *change catalyst* for the change is the player taking ultimate responsibility for the change and who typically becomes the symbolic focus for the change.

This key player is also supplemented by, first of all, some 'change agent' whose role is to fire up managers with new ideas. In the cases in Part Two, this role was played by a consultant in Dowty Case, by a cadre of internal managers at Prudential (although some additional stimulus was provided by a consultant) and at ICL by internal specialists.

Although this highlights the use of 'consultants', these do not, by any means, have to be 'external'. Ideally, change is fired up from within — but often the skills required to drive change proactively may not be plentiful. Even where internal players do have the skills to play this role effectively, they may either a) be at middle levels in the organisation and be afraid of damaging their career chances, or b) be too senior and be afraid of losing their roles or status or indeed be seen as having 'hidden political agendas'. Only where the chief executive gives (either overtly or covertly) the change agent some sort of 'protective shield' from attack will he be able to exercise his difficult role effectively. This may also include some implicit suggestion that his/her future career prospects will be enhanced by success in the role — bearing in mind the obvious increased risk surrounding the change agent role.

> The *change agent* is an external or internal player whose task
> is to start up the change process.

The external change agent, too, may need to think about his/her own resilience in the face of potential challenge within the organisation. He/she may be threatened by resistances from certain players in an organisation which may emerge, sometimes subtly, sometimes unsubtly. The question then arises: 'how independent is the external facilitator?' — especially if he works over several months almost wholly with one client. A good rule of thumb is for the consultant to ensure that he or she does not draw more than 50 per cent of his/her revenue from a single client over any rolling six-month period. It is unwise to become a 'pet change agent'; even when the consultant is far from being tame by nature.

Easing-in and exiting the players

Coming back now to the roles which the players may execute in the change process, Figure 3.3 highlights how these may change over time. This figure illustrates how:

- The catalyst (usually the chief executive or managing director) will gradually reduce his involvement in the change process — but at the very front end of the change he/she is the key player.
- The change agent is typically eased-into his position by the catalyst and plays a prominent and important role in the early stage of change.
- But even at early stages there is a need for a 'steering agent' to work

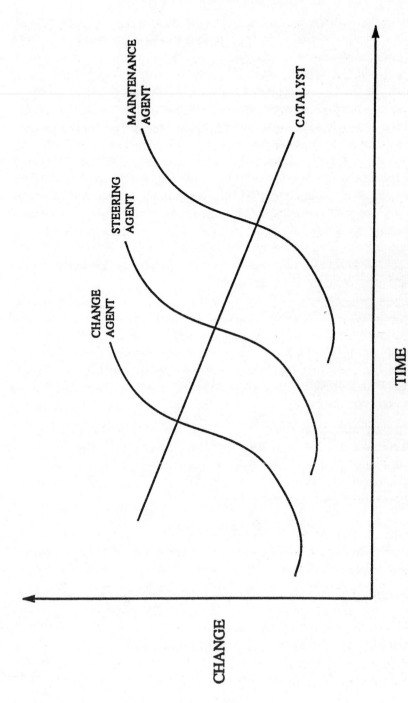

Figure 3.3 Phases of change

in parallel with the change agent to channel the change. The *steering agent* can be defined as the agent whose task is to ensure that, once a change initiative is up and running, it does not get diverted or lose momentum in its later stages. This can be done in a 'project manager role'. (In the Dowty case in Chapter 5 this role was executed by the business development director. In Chapter 6 this role was executed at the Prudential by the newly appointed project manager co-ordinating change initiatives.)

- Towards the end of the first phase of implementation of change (Stage 3 of our previous model), the steering agent comes to the fore and the 'change agent' may withdraw gradually, or perhaps suddenly, from the scene. It may be argued that few facilitators are equally good at 'firing up' with new ideas and also in focusing the more detailed implementation of change. (The exit of the consultant at Dowty occurred gradually over a three-month period as the management team took over all steering activities.)

- Next, as the change itself becomes more or less well channelled and implementation requires 'more of the same' rather than continual review and questioning of rationale and process, the 'maintenance agent' can take over. Typically this is a less challenging political task than that posed by the previous roles, but is nevertheless vital to ensure an effective role out of change. It also involves increasing tenacity and patience.

> The *maintenance agent* is a player whose task is to follow through the (routine) process of change through routine roll-out in the organisation or through providing effort to sustain it in the long term.

CASE EXERCISE

For a major change in your business, who were the key players and what roles did they play (catalyst, change agent, steering agent, maintenance agent)? Did some players try to exercise more than one role and how did this work out?

Sustaining the change — the long haul

Within this model the 'catalyst' (chief executive or managing director) is depicted as withdrawing gradually from up-front involvement. We should make some cautionary points here, however. This may be perceived (erroneously) as the catalyst becoming switched-off and disinterested. During this later phase key stakeholders who resented the change originally, but have gone underground, appearing to go along positively with the change, may resurface and move into more active resistance. No sooner than the chief executive, the change agent and the steering agent believe that 'the old paradigm is dead', certain elements may therefore resurface and threaten to come to the fore. This problem may be aptly called the 'decoy syndrome'. Figure 3.3 paints an idealised picture which, though useful, may not be reflected in practice.

Another key question is what parameters to put on the time axis for Figure 3.3. In many cases of organisational change of a less tangible nature one should follow the old adage of 'think of a number and double it' in estimating timescales. Typical scales quoted for achieving a fundamental shift in organisational paradigms run as follows:

- implementing quality — 3-5 years;
- a change intervention to reshape management culture — 4-6 or more years.

Clearly, these timescales may be compressed in special circumstances. For instance, had Hanson succeeded in buying ICI we may have seen a much more rapid change in ICI's 'paradigm'. But this would have been achieved at some cost: although change would be greatly compressed, this would not be achieved without fundamentally damaging the organisational culture.

When consultants quote such long timescales for managing softer areas of change, most senior managers respond with horror. Managers may suspect that the consultants' main motivation is to keep themselves going on a 'nice little earner' for a long time, and it is certainly a valid point for managers and consultants alike to watch out for over-dependency (both ways) which can develop incrementally and imperceptibly. However, some areas of change (especially those active at the core of the organisational paradigm) do seem to take years to work through. But this does not mean that change cannot be accelerated. The main value of external consultants acting as change agents may be to accelerate the speed and to increase the ease of change. This contrasts with a more traditional view that strategic change consulting is primarily geared to setting the strategic direction — although this may be an important role in kick-starting change.

Getting lost — the case of 'workshop-aholia'

Some caveats are now put on the whole concept of change interventions. Key players in a major change can become absorbed in its process and as 'there seems to be a lot happening', there is a feeling of tangible progress and success. This can degenerate into a kind of 'workshop-aholia' where each week is packed with workshops surfacing issues, testing behaviour and formulating action plans, but where real and tangible benefits may seem illusive. It is also a good idea to beware the 'changaholics' — those staff who see managing change as an attractive new industry and who tout for opportunities to run change programmes for their own sake. An important discipline, therefore, is to have continual reviews to test what value is being delivered by the change. This may involve continually questioning what key insights have emerged, what behaviour shifts have occurred, what initiatives have been started and, equally, what initiatives have been finished and with what benefit.

Without regular checks against milestones for strategic change, the 'intended' or 'deliberate' change strategy (to paraphrase Mintzberg, 1978) may become unrealised. Where 'change' embraces many less tangible areas it may be wise to focus on 'indicators' rather than precise measures in establishing progress towards achieving change objectives.

> These *milestones* can be defined as those key events which signal that some of the targeted results of change have been realised, or that a step towards achieving these results has been attained.

Tied up in the loops of change

Even where the process is designed to embrace all the most critical organisational systems which are 'in play' as a result of the change, there may be some more peripheral areas which remain unaffected. These 'systems' have been graphically called 'loops of strategic change' (Boogon and Komocar, 1990) — for example, rewards systems.

> *Loops of strategic change* are those interconnected parts of the

organisation which interact as a system to either mobilise for or build up resistance to change.

Key players in the intervention therefore need to ask themselves:

- Have we identified all the major loops of strategic change which impact on this change?
- How are these loops likely to interact as a system — for example, rewards systems may reinforce short-term behaviour which might thwart implementation of a strategic plan?
- Are we managing these effectively and which ones are likely to take more sustained effort to modify?
- Are there any more 'minor' loops which we also need to manage proactively? For example, recruitment activity may seem small but have a continuous impact on an organisation's ability to manage with international vision.
- Have we reached critical mass in our change efforts in each and every one of these loops?

As an example, in one strategic review it seemed as if the change team had genuinely tackled all of the key 'loops of strategic change' — from strategic direction, operational practices, rewards and recognition through to management culture. However, despite major successes on all of these fronts, the process of change faltered. But what had happened? Looking back, some key 'change loops' had not been addressed effectively, particularly in terms of securing the backing of the group for the scale and cost of necessary change. This also highlights the need for the change agent not to assume that the managing director and his team will actually drive through planned change with similar vigour to that which they have espoused in the strategic plan.

The idea of 'change systems' is amplified further in Chapter 4, which focuses on specific analysis tools of change.

CASE EXERCISE

For a particular change you have been involved in or are currently involved in: what are the key organisational systems which your change impacts on a) directly and b) indirectly? How is this (was this) reflected in the change plan? What less obvious systems impact on the change but were not or are not taken into account and with what result?

Let us now look at a short hypothetical case on 'how *not* to do it', which highlights the need to understand how any change process needs to be positioned in order to achieve sustainable benefits.

Short case on change workshops — Euroflop

A consultant was asked to present his plans for a 'Managing Change' workshop programme to a group of managers in a major European company, Euroflop. The brief was to present a proposal for how to shift the capability of a number of middle managers in managing change.

The consultant argued that, based on his experience, a programme lasting a minimum of several days, including a number of change projects, would be needed to begin to unfreeze the mind-sets and behaviours of managers. He warned that this was a *de minimis* approach — to achieve a significant and sustainable shift in attitudes and behaviour it would be necessary to arrange for follow-through to some live 'change activities'. In turn, the success of the programme would be heavily influenced by the visible and active involvement of senior management.

The Euroflop managers did not seem to be entirely happy with these ideas and there seemed to be a major gap between what they had espoused — 'we want to run some change programmes' — and what they were actually prepared to cope with. Take, for example the following interchange where what is said is in standard type and what is being thought is in italics. The consultant has just introduced his proposal for a change programme which deals with a number of topical issues.

Consultant: You asked me who these programmes should be for? It is my understanding that you are targeting these at 'middle managers'. However, I do think that you must involve senior people to really position the programme. Yes, some senior input is absolutely vital and not just a symbolic blessing.

                     I am really understating this, there is no way that we can do this for real without their central input.

EF Manager 1:   I can see problems in getting senior people involved in this.

                     Oh dear, there is no way that the general manager will be involved in another course.

EF Manager 2:   You asked about 'what change issues we wanted to focus on'. Well we can't really tell you anything specific. This is really a . . . kind of . . . well, we just want people to get a feel that . . . well change is happening faster than we seem to be coping with it.

I really liked that book by Rosabeth Moss Kanter and I think these people should really know about it.

Consultant: Are you saying that really there is nothing specific that you want the programme to deal with?

They really don't seem to have much concrete idea about what this is and what it entails. I feel I am on quicksand.

EF Manager 2:   Well yes, I mean, we really are quite successful relative to the companies you have dealt with previously (referring to the consultant's overhead which included several major blue-chip companies which were, by and large, relatively successful). I don't really feel there is a major push for change within our company.

Can't he just see that we are very successful — we just need the issue of change to be covered.

EF Manager 3:   I think I saw it as mainly a conceptual training programme.

I don't like the sound of all this behavioural stuff one bit.

Consultant: Well, I am afraid I don't fully agree. You see, OK there is a conceptual element and that's what most of the change tools are aimed at. But the flipside is behaviour. I see this as being equally behavioural.

I have never forgotten my experience with that major blue chip company, XYZ, who saw change as cerebral and tried to take me to pieces when we went outside the safe land of hard analysis.

EF Manager 3: I don't really see why we can't do this in one day?

This will get rid of him.

Consultant: Believe me, I am never one to inflate a consulting project — that's why I don't still work for ABC Management Consultants. But it honestly does take a day at least to thaw people out and then a day of constructive reflection to analyse your own change issues. If you want to halve the investment, the benefits will be a quarter or less, maybe negative . . .

I am really sure now they don't want this at all, but let's just force this out.

EF Manager 2: My problem is that it will have to compete with our other training courses. I mean, we are having strategic management from Cranridge and leadership from Henfield, and quality from Moonbridge Park, I am worried about duplication, or even triplication.

All those wonderfully nice things we are doing . . .

EF Manager 4: And I am worried that they might like it so much (the pilot group) that everyone will want to go on it.

We could really do some good work here but how can we possibly cope with it?

Consultant: That sounds like success and helping achieve 'critical mass' to me.

Maybe this will chink their armour?

EF Manager 5: Isn't it possible to go on one of your public programmes to try it out?

Let's put up a hurdle and see if he can jump over it.

Consultant: Unfortunately you have just missed the last one, the next is in six months' time.

This risk aversion is beginning to get to me.

EF Manager 5:   Well, if this programme is so marvellous, how come you only run these so infrequently?

Now is the time to pounce — that will fix him!

Consultant: So infrequently, hum, well these kinds of programmes only really run every six months. I am beginning to think that we are seeing here a solution in search of a problem. It seems to me that you have a number of choices here, either you genuinely seize the opportunity of making this programme really have organisational impact or you more or less do nothing. But if you really think that 'managing change' is just another training course, well ... it hardly puts you at any kind of 'leading edge' which is where I saw you as originally coming from. But I will accept that some organisations are just not quite ready for this kind of thing. It needs some kind of leap into it — you can't just sit at the edge of the pool thinking should we/ shouldn't we — you know, dive in, it is either all or nothing.

A classic case of what people espouse they want being totally different from what they want or need. I will be well out of here shortly.

The Euroflop case underlines the importance of focusing on targeted benefits (whether tangible or less tangible) rather than simply on a 'nice thing to be seen to be doing'. It also highlights that many internal staff want to be 'seen to be doing something' about facilitating change, but have not really begun to think through the implications of changing the organisational paradigm — a potentially risky activity. To commence a neutered change programme would raise artificial expectations which can only lead to failure, followed by a substantial fall-out of cynicism. The consultant may have been wise to avoid a half-baked intervention.

Not all readers will want to or can afford to employ consultants, so an important topic is 'how to run a change workshop'. A learning curve is involved in setting workshop agenda and process. It may be worthwhile to get all our readers up to speed by posing a number of questions on 'how to run a change workshop' before moving on to the topic of people and capability.

How to run a change workshop — twelve key questions

- What is the objective of the workshop?
- How does it relate to other initiatives?
- What do we see as the key outputs (learning, problem definition, action plans, behavioural shift, etc) and how will these be documented and communicated, and to whom?
- Who needs to be involved?
- How will it be positioned in the organisation and by whom?
- Who will facilitate and are they seen as competent and impartial?
- Where should it be held and what facilities are required?
- What are the next steps following the workshop likely to be?
- What key barriers and blockages may arise and how will these be dealt with and by whom?
- What specific activities will be undertaken and what inputs will this require?
- How will these be broken down into discussion groups and who will be in each one?
- How long is required to make substantial progress on each issue and what happens if tasks are incomplete?

Experience shows that it is essential to consider all these questions at length, rather than rushing into a workshop on a particular issue with merely a broad agenda. The questions emphasise both content *and* process, and involve thinking through how these interrelate. They also involve analysing both current and future context — this provides high quality feed-in of data and also helps to think through feed-back into the management process in detail and in advance.

Where you are dealing with a sensitive issue(s) in a workshop, it is advisable to set up some ground rules for interaction. One method is to write key words on flipcharts beginning with 'P': things to avoid will include being political, picky, procrastinating, pedantic, whilst things to practise are being positive. Having set up these process rules there is, typically, very little need to refer to them. When this is done, tension can be diffused through a good dose of humour.

CASE EXERCISE

For a change issue which you are currently facing, using the twelve key questions earlier, design (on one sheet of A4) a framework for a one-day workshop drawing on the above checklist.

PEOPLE AND CAPABILITY

The people element

We have already considered organisational capability in Chapter 2. Increasingly, the capability of individuals is being seen (at least by theorists and in the world of conferences) as a critical dimension in competitive advantage. What is not obvious is whether this is reflected in actual management practice. Before turning to the realities of management, however, let us examine a useful model from Ulrich and Lake (1990) who contrast traditional sources of competitive advantage with 'softer' areas.

Traditional sources (according to Ulrich and Lake) include:

- economic/financial capability;
- strategic/marketing capability;
- technological capability.

  Organisational capability is thus defined as an organisation's capability to respond flexibly, effectively and quickly to its environment with least apparent effort.

Capability development

In the final analysis, underlying organisational capability is one of the few sources of unique advantage available to businesses. According to Ulrich and Lake, organisational capability enables a business to adapt to changing customer and competitive needs. Thus, a crucial part of organisational capability is flexibility in implementing change. Yet, so many organisations with their still rigid or semi-rigid hierarchies, with their incessant and unproductive politics and attention to procedural rituals seem designed to undermine that capability.

Personnel departments may play a major role in contributing to this inflexibility and loss of value. The effect of this was captured by the managing director of a management buy-out team whose business was bought out from a large group:

> Personnel played a classic role in making life more bureaucratic. They had (he begins to laugh) a vested interest in creating a tall structure so that they could worry themselves and others about manpower planning, management development, job descriptions and assessment of potential.

This is echoed by an organisational change consultant:

> I once helped a company save £10m per year simply by taking out the bulk of the personnel function. This saved £5m in direct costs but at least £5m of value we calculated was added each year by avoiding the indirect costs of inflexibility that they (personnel) caused throughout the organisation.

Fortunately, things are beginning to change, although at an uneven pace. For instance, the human resources director of a retailer said recently that in his view:

> Over the past ten years, the whole personnel management scene has changed. We used to be pre-occupied, so obsessed, by industrial relations issues and personnel procedures. Now we are beginning to grapple with genuinely creating competitive advantage through empowering people — but it is a steep upward hill.

But besides fashionable 'things to do' such as empowerment, some of the most useful areas for action in improving organisational capability may come from relatively simple measures, for example:

- Control the number, complexity and style of management meetings. In larger organisations these are usually the main drain on time and energies.
- Simplify communication: if it cannot be said on two or three sheets of A4 paper does it need to be said at all?
- Avoid false hare races: exercise tight control over any new initiative as commitment to it will rapidly snowball.

- Regularly review change activities to see 'what should be concluded', to avoid unnecessary clutter and overload.

CASE EXERCISE

What are the five key weaknesses which undermine organisational capability in your company? What are the adverse effects on performance? What key change thrusts might address these problems?

Another major factor which undermines organisational capability is the insidious effect of myopic business analysis or 'MBA-thinking' as propagated by many business schools. Particular culprits include:

- Incremental thinking about change projects. These may be looked at in isolation in terms of their operational and organisational impact and also in trying to assess net financial benefits less costs with precision. Incremental thinking emphasises analysis of business often at the expense of synthesis . Through understanding the whole and interdependencies between parts of the change issues facing a business (synthesis) it is possible to reach different conclusions about what should be given highest priority.
- Viewing change problems and opportunities in primarily functional as opposed to cross-functional terms.
- Espousing the need for a trade-off between long- and shorter-term performance without identifying methods through which managers can avoid focusing purely on the short-term in their behaviour.

For more on the important topic of the drawbacks of incremental thinking in business, see recent books by Senge (1990) and by Grundy (1992). Suffice it to say that myopic business analysis ('MBA-thinking') is a major factor undermining efforts to improve organisational capability in the 1990s. 'Analysis' is important but is insufficient. On its own, it may conspire to undermine rather than strengthen organisational capability.

A classic case of incremental thinking is the urge by accountants to question the benefits of training and development. This is countered by the equal but opposite desire of many human resource developers to protect training and development from business and financial appraisal. The arguments may quickly get bogged down in spurious claims about whether (and how) benefits can be quantified over and above simply doing no training and development at all.

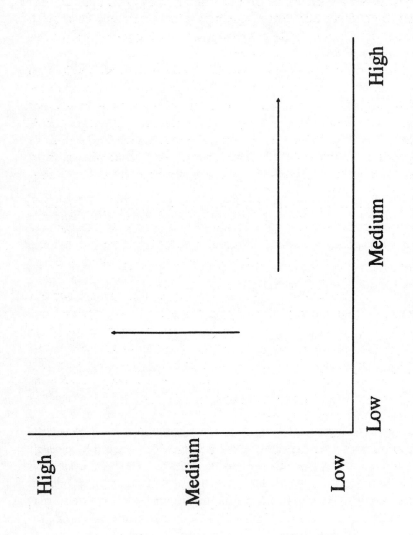

Figure 3.4 Willingness and capability

Yet, without any training and development a gradual decline in capability may set in. This may be because existing managers are not revitalised, high fliers may leave, and new blood may not be easy to attract. In short, without effective and relevant training and development, capability and performance may decline.

But training and development activities on their own are unlikely to strengthen, let alone sustain, capability. Unless an organisation provides appropriate organisational climate and support for new management skills and style, much investment in training and development is squandered. This highlights the need to take into account a number of inter-dependencies between key parts of the organisational system to understand the sustainable benefits of using management development as a vehicle for change.

As a final contribution to this debate on capability, Figure 3.4 enables managers to plot the relative willingness and capability (to change) for key players. The point of this matrix is that not all players will be capable of making the change happen, either because they are overloaded or haven't got the skills or are disorganised. There is also the question of 'willingness', which may vary: someone may be capable of changing but not willing, or equally might be willing to change but not capable.

This matrix is useful as it separates out skills issues from more behavioural issues so that training for change can be more focused. It also helps to avoid situations where an inappropriate mix of people is thrown together to implement change. Where a number of managers are both relatively unwilling to change and are less than fully capable, a major obstacle to change is in the making.

In the next chapter we will see a similar (although different) matrix dealing with stakeholders in terms of relative power and attitude toward the change.

CASE EXERCISE

Within your own department, what is a) the willingness of key members of staff to change, and b) their capability? What strategies does this suggest for reducing resistances and for developing capability?

MANAGING EXPECTATIONS AND COMMUNICATION

Expecting the unexpected

Managing expectations is a critical part of preparing the organisation for change — both in terms of the quantity of change and also its type or 'quality'. Unless expectations are raised that change will occur, the resistances to change will be much greater. On the other hand, if

---

Areas which need to be considered:

- The degree of advanced disclosure of the change. This should include what is 'closed' and what is still 'open'. Disclosure will add to full 'diagnosis' as more data will be received on both the rationale of the change and also on barriers to implementation, but may set up barriers if handled badly.
- The detailed timetable is:
  - who to talk to?
  - about what?
  - when?
  - in what order?
- Structuring the medium:
  - company circular (cheap but possibly ineffective)
  - large group (quick but represses feedback)
  - small groups (slow but gives better feedback)
  - think about what to do (if anything) about the people who will be left out.
- Structuring the message:
  - be clear, simple and consistent
  - think through the 'perceived implications'
  - talk about the downsides openly but emphasise the upsides
- Think about the likely response:
  - allow time to absorb the message
  - be prepared to deal with shock
  - empathise with the impact which you know it will have

Note: Figure 3.5 is indebted to Estelle Bowman, The Management College, Henley.

Figure 3.5 Formulating a communication plan

expectations are raised too much or at too early a stage, this will create and aggravate a sense of disappointment.

> *Expectations management* can thus be defined as the shaping of beliefs about what will happen and how it will happen as a result of a change process, and to whom and when.

It is essential, therefore, to have a well thought out communications plan to manage expectations which will achieve just the right level of stimulation at the right time (see Figure 3.5).

> *Communication* can thus be defined as the channelling of information about the change top-down, bottom-up or horizontally within an organisation and also externally.

Open communication is by no means an easy task. The temptation is to proceed with change with any negative connotations in a covert way. Equally, where there are major positive benefits anticipated from the change, there may be a temptation to over-sell the benefits. Also, management might be over-optimistic that they will reap the benefits at a relatively early stage. Where the change is major and fundamental - for example, a quality programme — the beneficial effects may be felt in earnest some years rather than a few months into the process. Unless expectations of the duration of change are managed — particularly when the first benefits might be expected — there is likely to be a steep drop in organisational self-esteem and performance. This patience needs to be balanced against the need for some targeting of change benefits.

CASE EXERCISE

For a change that you are currently facing: use Figure 3.5 to draw up an outline communication plan. How will initial communication be followed up and how will you ensure that there is two-way communication?

'Managing expectations' also invites the question of managing whose expectations? It is essential to identify and evaluate the key stakeholders in the change. This is covered in Chapter 4 on Change Tools. The pool of 'stakeholders' may change during the change process. For this reason, it is necessary to keep the communication plan constantly under review.

CASE EXERCISE

For a change you are currently involved in: how are you managing the expectations of those affected either directly or indirectly by that change? Does this include not only the final outcome of change but also the change process itself? What specific steps can you take in order to reshape expectations (for example, through meetings, surveys, workshops, conferences, etc) to set a more appropriate level of expectations?

Anticipating the pain — organisational yoga

Another important dimension is the need to manage negative expectations. For instance, when the change involves some element of re-structuring or down-sizing it is important to be clear in communicating its scope and probable impact (in broadest terms), together with the rationale for the change. This may seem counter-intuitive at first sight. Many managers may instinctively wish to opt for 'keeping managers in the dark' or 'making sure that their noses are at the grindstone'. Often, this is unrealistic as organisations are 'leaky' so far as information is concerned. The 'stories' which begin to circulate may exaggerate the impact of the change and actually do more damage than would the truth.

Where the need for restructuring and down-sizing is either periodic or ongoing — in both cases posing a continual drain on morale — it is helpful to link this to 'the change rationale'. Although not necessarily alleviating the pain of change, this should diffuse the hostility which managers focus on their bosses. Many senior managers often feel uncomfortable talking publicly and openly about the impact of competitive and financial pressures on the business, and its implications for organisational change. This is rather like the captain of a ship not wanting to convey news of a pending storm for fear of upsetting the cosy climate in the ship's mess (possibly leading to the ship being abandoned prematurely).

Inevitably, many changes will involve some degree of pain and it is wise to prepare the 'patient' for some discomfort. For instance, top management may extol the virtues of 'culture change' without emphasising that some individuals will find it difficult to adjust their style to being more open, and that this involves letting go of the trappings of status. Alternatively, where everyone knows that down-sizing is in the offing, a useful lubricant of change is to continue with management development programmes in order to upgrade staff skills. This may assist them in the marketplace for jobs, and for those that stay, give a feeling that, although times are tough, the company cares.

Managing upwards

Before we leave the topic of communication , it is worth emphasising that upward communication can be a powerful tool for change. This can be channelled by employee attitude surveys which are likely to reveal difficulties and contradictions in management style and communication. This may provide powerful input into the message that change is essential.

Communicating externally

Another approach is to use external media to amplify the change message. We see this applied in the case of one major company's culture change programme, where intimate details of the early formulation of the strategy were published prominently and simultaneously with internal communication in the press. Corporate image programmes may also be used to the same effect — their principal target may be employees rather than customers or shareholders.

CONCLUSION

Change is a dynamic process which needs to be anticipated, shaped and controlled. As change progresses, the perceptions of 'things going well' or 'not so well' in the organisation will invariably shift. This is also associated (with lags) with dips in performance which may be inevitable, but may, however, be minimised through effective change management. The depth and duration of these dips in performance are influenced greatly by the way in which the change is communicated. A robust communication strategy needs to take into account what and how much will be communicated, when, to whom and from whom, and through what media. It will also be of great benefit if the process is genuinely two-way, that it involves listening and learning by senior management and a preparedness to adjust change plans where appropriate. More coercive strategies for change are unlikely to achieve commitment of staff, and will involve less tangible costs such as defining morale, 'psychological quitting' or giving up.

Relative effectiveness in managing change is highlighted by the five stage model of diagnosis, planning, implementation, control and learning. This model can reveal deficiencies in past change management, while also serving as a tool for balancing and refocusing future efforts. The model also emphasises the crucial ingredient of effective leadership to steer change to its goals.

When beginning any major change, the scope, focus and style of any intervention need careful planning. Interventions can and should be re-shaped as the change process progresses — highlighting the need for flexible change intervention strategies. The game plan of who will be involved in leading and shaping the change also needs to be well thought through in advance. Particular attention should be paid to how the intervention can reach critical mass and, once there, how it can be sustained.

A major factor underpinning the success or failure of any change is underlying organisational capability. Besides being a critical part of an organisation's competitive advantage, organisational capability reflects its inherent flexibility, adaptiveness and capacity to retain coherence and focus, despite external and internal pressures. Change strategies may be aimed at building organisational capability or they may unwittingly destroy it. Equally, the process of change itself will be accelerated or greatly retarded depending on that capability.

Lastly, expectations play a major role in mobilising and shaping change. They can also conspire to block change where undue or premature expectations have been raised (beware the 'hype' factor in packaging initiatives to implement strategic change). Where the change involves major pain, it may be unwise to pretend this does not exist, setting up future expectations that the change will be pain-free. This leads on to the importance of devising a detailed communication plan. This may follow a variety of strategies depending on the context and content of change — and also the preferred style of the key players.

The change process is, therefore, amenable to analysis, design and focusing. Combined with the tools for change discussed in the next chapter, this account of the change process gives the practising manager a potential edge in being able to implement strategic change. Up to now, this advantage has been elusive in the many books on leadership, strategy and organisational theory.

4

POWER TOOLS FOR CHANGE

TOOLING UP FOR THE TASK

This chapter contains a wide range of tools for analysing change issues, planning and controlling the implementation of change and, finally, for learning. Although some of these tools are old and some relatively new, their age is less important than their effectiveness.

Each tool can be used (at least initially) on its own. Indeed, it is advised that the practising manager begins by experimenting with just one tool to get its feel and to gain some measure of confidence before experimenting with other tools. Typically, what will happen is that the tool will have been found useful, but there may be some issues which might just have to be teased out with another change tool.

Should this occur, it is advised that you cast around to see if one of the other change tools may be of use. For example, you may have identified key 'enablers and constraints' using a force field analysis (see later section) but may feel that these are incomplete as you have not addressed fully the 'key stakeholders'.

A step-by-step approach to 'trying out the power tools' on a selective basis is, therefore, advised. Many purveyors of management tools (including some business schools) seek to shower the practising manager with 'frameworks' and 'concepts' and 'tools' without regard for the learning rate of managers. Even where managers are intellectually superhuman, they still need time to practise and reflect on the use of the tools, as well as an opportunity to reinforce their learning with further practice. Unless a tool is fully internalised (and most managers can cope with experimenting perhaps at most with two or three at once), it is highly unlikely that they will sustain their use back at the coal face for any length of time.

Although it is wise to be selective in the choice of tools to experiment with, the ambitious manager will seek familiarity, if not fluency, in all four tools which include:

- force field analysis;
- change systems;
- stakeholder analysis;
- change project management.

The above tools can also be used in conjunction with the paradigm (see Chapter 2) as illustrated in Figure 4.1 and also competitive benchmarking. This shows how an internal paradigm shift can influence the change objective. Analysis of the existing paradigm is also useful in gaining an understanding of the tangible and less tangible forces that have an impact on the change process. Further, change systems provide a useful checklist to ensure that the key systems of change have been incorporated within the force field analysis. Finally, stakeholder analysis identifies the most influential and powerful stakeholders who may support or block change. A truly robust force field analysis draws inputs from all of these sources. We, therefore, turn first to force field analysis.

FORCE FIELD ANALYSIS

Surfacing the forces

Force field analysis is perhaps the oldest and certainly the most established of the power tools for change. This tool was devised by Lewin (1935) who also contributed the idea of 'unfreezing' as a phase in managing change. Force field analysis can be defined as follows:

> *Force field analysis* is the diagnosis and evaluation of enabling and restraining forces that have an impact on the change process.

Force field analysis is a tool which brings to the surface the underlying forces which may pull a particular change forward or which may prevent

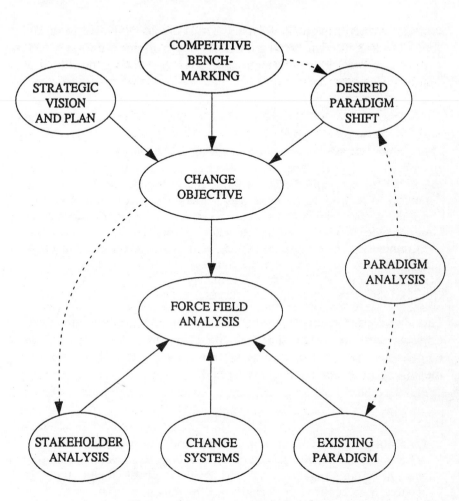

Figure 4.1   Integrating the tools

progress, or even move the change backwards. These 'forces' can be separately identified as 'enablers' or 'constraints'. But neither set of forces can be adequately identified without first specifying the change objective.

> The *change objective* is where you want to be or need to be, suggesting a gap with where you are now.

Defining the change objective (and the change gap) is an important and interesting task. Changes are often implemented with relatively fuzzy and sometimes inconsistent objectives. The change objective should be defined to link into the strategic vision for the organisation (where it is a major project), its operational objectives and to organisational and financial goals.

CASE EXAMPLE

In a two-day change workshop involving middle managers in a large service company, the issue of the re-organisation of the sales force came up. Participants realised that they were not just a little unclear but very unclear as to why this re-organisation was being conducted. Was it to achieve greater market focus, closeness to the customer, to reduce costs or to juggle existing managers into different slots? The managers seemed to remember the original intentions of the change project, but these appear to have been overlaid with ambitions of new stakeholders with the result of lost direction and focus for the change.

The above case example underlines the need to define the change objective and to ensure that the change is project managed. It also emphasises that existing and new stakeholders' aspirations and needs must be skilfully managed and balanced.

CASE EXERCISE

For a change issue with which you are currently dealing, what do you see as being the central change objective? How does this link (if at all) with strategic vision, organisational and financial goals? Where there is apparently more than one change objective, how important are the sub-objectives relative to one another? Is it possible to achieve one but not the other(s)? To what extent are they in conflict and if so how can this be managed?

Turning back now to force field analysis, the most effective way of evaluating the forces enabling or constraining achievement of the change objective is to do so pictorially in a force field diagram. This diagram represents the relative strength of each individual change force by drawing an arrowed line whose length is in proportion to that relative strength.

For ex-scientists and mathematicians, force field analysis may be

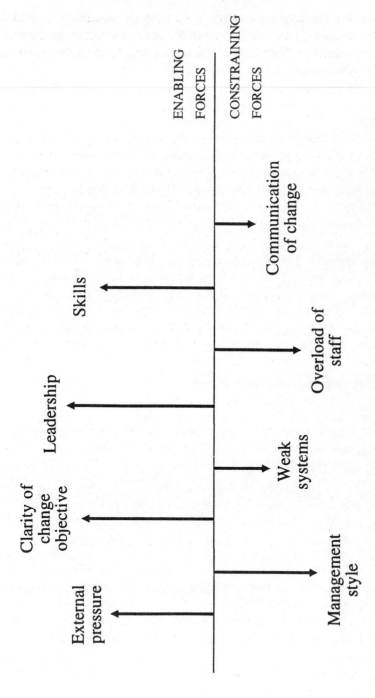

Figure 4.2 Force field analysis

reminiscent of both vector analysis and also Newton's laws of mechanics. This resemblance is no coincidence, for change is a dynamic process involving a number of influences akin to physical forces both within and outside the organisation. The beauty of force field analysis lies in making less tangible influences in change more tangible and measurable and also in capturing influences of an indirect nature. When combined with tangible forces, this presents a complete vision (at least in snap-shot form) of the influences acting on the change.

A horizontal version of a generic force field analysis is depicted in Figure 4.2. Note in this case that, on balance, the 'enabling' forces appear stronger than the constraining forces. The horizontal version of force field analysis has the merit of graphically highlighting this relative balance. Some managers prefer to draw their force field analysis vertically, with enabling forces moving to the right and constraining forces to the left. This vertical version has the merit of being easier to write on a flipchart as the force 'headings' can be written up without being bunched together. However, the power of highlighting the 'change balance' is defeated or lost with vertical formats (few managers are prepared actually to lie down horizontally to see what the overall balance of forces really looks like).

What force field analysis is not

Before we move on to the more detailed mechanics of identifying and evaluating the forces and to applications of force field analysis, a few caveats are needed. First, managers can become confused between force field analysis and cost/benefit analysis. Force field analysis is not a form of cost/benefit analysis: it does not purport to analyse whether the content of the change, particularly the outputs, is of great value or not. This issue should be resolved in defining the rationale of change. Force field analysis takes the overall direction and intent of the change process (at least initially) as a given. It asks 'given that X or Y is the change objective, what key enablers or constraining forces may impact on progress to meet that objective?' It is thus concerned, above all, with change process rather than with change outputs.

Force field analysis is also not to be confused with analysis of external competitive environment per se or the position of a particular business. Where managers encounter force field analysis in the same workshop programme as Porter's five competitive forces or 'SWOT' analysis, this can inadvertently confuse them when they meet force field analysis which is essentially a device for mapping the change process.

Managing objections to force field analysis

Managers who are 'content-led' in their management style may now feel like objecting 'so what?' to the idea of force field analysis. Partly, this is a reflection of many managers being inattentive to getting the management process right and being primarily 'results-driven'. Although to some extent the influence of the 'quality' management philosophy has made inroads into a 'results' and 'output-driven' mentality, there is clearly a long way to go in many European and Western organisations in giving due attention to injecting quality into the management process.

Force field analysis can highlight constraints which were previously fuzzy or submerged and which when surfaced can appear daunting (if not alarming). One way of forcing constraints to the surface is, first of all, to get managers to work on a 'difficult change case'. A useful tip is to use a well known problem, such as that of 'Managing Change at British Rail' as a case example, because British Rail has faced a difficult set of constraints. This use of a case from another company (with which managers can quickly get to grips) amplifies the message of a force field analysis, where change is seen as being particularly difficult to implement.

What force field analysis captures

It is now time to take a closer look at the kinds of forces which are typically captured within the force field analysis. These include both tangible and less tangible forces, and also forces with both direct and indirect influence. They may also include forces which are external to the organisation — for example, the impact of competitive market pressure which might increase the perceived need to change.

Figure 4.3 (which should be read vertically rather than horizontally) identifies key headings which should be considered when identifying the key forces.

Figure 4.2 is not necessarily complete: other and more specific influences will be uncovered on application of the force field method to a particular context.

It is worthwhile re-emphasising that unless the change objective is clearly specified, the force field analysis will become unfocused and non-

Tangible	*Less Tangible*
Sufficiency of resources	Leadership
Sufficiency of time	Communication
People skills	Clarity of change objectives and strategy for achieving these
Supporting systems	Backing of influential stakeholders
Market & competitive pressure	Employee commitment
Financial pressure	Links to other reinforcing areas of change
Project management process in place	Participation by staff in change planning
Clear deliverables	Corporate backing

Figure 4.3   Key areas of enabling or constraining forces

specific. This re-emphasises the importance of the diagnosis phase, particularly that concerned with specifying the problem, need or opportunity which the change seeks to address.

Interpreting the results

The next problem which often arises is deciding whether a specific force is an 'enabler' or a 'constraint' and, in both cases, how powerful this force is. In some instances, this is not obvious and managers become frustrated to find that what promised to be a 'nice, easy and simple tool to use' is fraught with apparent problems. In reality 'the problems' occur because the force field analysis tool forces managers into some hard thinking. What this usually means is not that there is something wrong with the tool, but that there is more than one force at work. It is possible to find more than one force intermingled in a particular area. For example, although market and competitive pressure may increase the sense of need for change, this may also reduce the organisation's capability to digest change. External pressure may reduce the amount of real and

84

perceived energy and resources to implement strategic change effectively. In that event, the force field analysis should show two forces — one enabling and another one constraining — so the original analysis becomes rich and may change organically.

The next issue that arises is how to evaluate the relative strength of the various forces. Two methods used successfully in the past include:

- scoring each force as having 'high', 'medium' or 'low' impact;
- scoring each force numerically on a scale of 1 to 5.

Most groups of managers work comfortably by using the high, medium or low scoring method. In exceptional cases (for example where managers have scientific backgrounds or have an inherent love of quantification) the 1 to 5 scale appears to fit more comfortably.

One of the common objections to force field analysis is that the whole scoring exercise is 'highly subjective'. This feeling normally occurs within the first ten minutes or so of any analysis exercise. It arises usually because all managers have done is to identify that a force is an enabler or a constraint without exploring questions including:

- Why is it *a force a particular* an enabler or a constraint?
- How important an influence is it on the change process (and when)?
- What underlying factors does it depend upon in turn?

This highlights that any force field analysis is dependent on many assumptions, many of which are implicit. A more successful and less 'subjective' analysis will have brought to the surface, shared and agreed these implicit assumptions.

A number of pitfalls need to be avoided in the use of force field analysis, which include:

- Focusing primarily on tangible (as opposed to less tangible) forces of change.
- Missing out major constraints because the team wishes to paint an 'ideal' rather than a realistic picture of the change.
- Failing to identify a 'stopper': that is, a change which has such a powerful impact that it is likely to stop the change in its tracks. 'Stoppers' should be drawn either as a thick black arrow or, alternatively, as an arrow which goes right to the bottom of the force field analysis and 'off the page'. (This assumes that you are using the vertical format for a force field analysis.)

A *stopper* can be defined as an influence or change which will effectively put an end to the initiative either through direct confrontation or passive resistance.

In addition to the above, there may be cases where a specific enabling force can be made strong and prove decisive in moving the change forward. This kind of force may be described as an 'unblocker' and can be drawn as a very long (or thick) positive line on the force field diagram.

There may also be instances where a negative and constraining force can be flipped over to make a positive force, and in so doing transform the picture. For instance, if an influential stakeholder (who is currently negative) can be turned around in favour of the change, this can provide a major driver in the change process.

The range of applications

Force field analysis can be applied for any area of change whether this is at the macro, micro or individual level. It can include, for example at the macro level, the successful integration of a major acquisition, interventions to shift organisational culture, decentralisation or organisational de-layering or major changes in systems or quality initiatives.

Force field analysis can also be used not merely within the diagnosis phase of change, but also in planning and in order to monitor and control implementation (the five-stage model in Chapter 3). At each phase of the change the incidence and relative influence of enablers and constraints will shift. This needs to be accommodated in change action plans. Lastly, it can also be used within the learning phase in order to re-appraise a (completed) change process and to distil lessons for future change and also for measuring underlying organisational capability.

Force field analysis is an active tool: it should be used not simply to reflect, but also to re-shape, change strategy and plans. At the diagnosis stage not only should it be used to map the existing pattern of change forces, but also to identify what pattern of forces is required in order to move the change forward at an acceptable pace. Frequently, managers relax exhausted or satiated by their analysis effort. The obvious application of force field analysis — to re-design the change to make it easier to implement — is all too often missed.

CASE EXERCISE

For a change which you are currently facing or about to deal with, what is the change objective? Given this objective, what are the key enablers and restraining forces impacting on the change process aimed at achieving that objective? What is the relative strength of these forces and what (overall) does the force field diagram look like? Are there any clues as to how this change can be re-shaped to make it easier or more feasible?

Force field analysis is, therefore, a core tool for managing change. Of all 'business school' tools it is possibly the most potent and is certainly the most undersold. Ideally, it should be used interactively in small groups, especially to gain proficiency. Once managers are proficient, however, it becomes easy to use it individually. Even when it is not used formally (in a force field picture) it is often found that the tool is used sub-consciously by managers, thus improving their intuitive thinking.

But force field analysis may uncover only a part of the change issues, and it is strongly advised that managers also consider using the other power tools, for example 'systems of change' to which we now turn. These other forces can provide 'feed-in' to the force field analysis and ensure not only that it is complete and fair, but also that all options for facilitating change have been explored.

A summary of the do's and don'ts of force field analysis

Do's include:

- Brainstorm all the key tangible and less tangible forces impacting on the change process.
- Include key forces drawn from your paradigm analysis, the analysis of key change systems and the stakeholder analysis.
- Test your judgements by questioning 'why?' a force is strong or weak by reference to the change objective and by thinking about its constraints within the change process.
- Do the initial force field analysis on an 'as is' basis — show the warts and be prepared to be provocative.
- Where a major constraint exists, draw this in as a stopper to draw attention to its role in braking the change process.

- Use the tool throughout the change process as the change forces will change over time.
- Involve others to provide input to the analysis and to test your views.

Don'ts include:

- Confuse force field analysis with simple cost-benefit analysis. Benefits should only be included as a force if they are perceived by and owned by key stakeholders. Often, these benefits are in the eye of the change initiator and are neutral in driving the change process forward.
- Use force field analysis as a tool just to describe the current position. Force field analysis should be used to re-shape actively your change plan to optimise the effect of enabling forces and to neutralise or flip-over the constraining forces to become enablers.
- Get bogged down in attempts to rate the forces precisely — force field analysis is a soft science.

SYSTEMS OF CHANGE

Expanding the vision

Change involves the interaction of a number of systems within an organisation. These may interact with one another in ways which will either facilitate or inhibit change. A key factor in managing change effectively is to understand how these systems interact with one another. Openness to understanding these interdependencies is identified by Senge (1990) as being a crucial part of 'the learning organisation'.

The 'systems of change' tool is derived from Peters' and Waterman's 'Five S's' which were explored in Chapter 2. The tool is depicted in Figure 4.4 as:

- strategy;
- structure;
- skills;
- systems;
- style.

Strategy appears at the core of the model in Figure 4.4. This signifies its co-ordinating role and also its role in direction-setting of change. What has been apparently 'dropped' are the two 'S's' which emphasise 'staff'

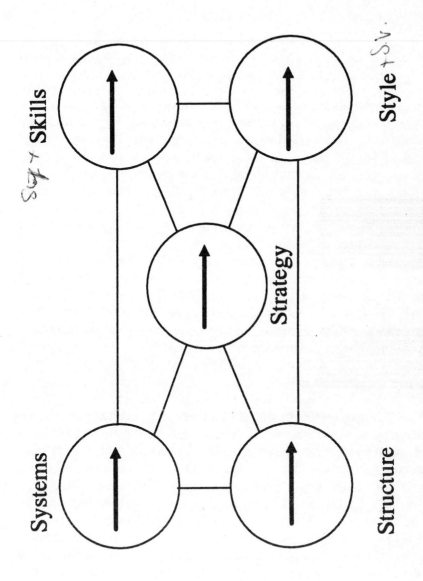

Figure 4.44 Change systems

and 'shared values'. This is in the interest of simplification, as to a certain extent 'staff' can be subsumed under 'skills' and 'shared values' under 'style'.

It is worthwhile to define 'style' at this point, as follows:

> *Style* is the *way* in which management acts thereby revealing its underlying attitudes, beliefs and values. It is concerned therefore with the *how* rather than with the *what* of action.

This model extends the earlier model of 'strategy, structure and culture'. Whilst the 'strategy, structure and culture' model is preferable for mapping the macro-level influences on strategic change at a more micro level, the 'five S's' model is more useful in identifying the specific influences on change. It also identifies their interaction, as well as the extent to which they are aligned or non-aligned in pursuit of a particular change.

Some of these 'ideal' linkages are not obvious when managers seek to implement change in practice. For instance, it would appear to be the exceptional organisation which has lined up its business strategy with its development plan for skills (and has also developed a responsive style). There are also immense practical difficulties in aligning systems with strategy. Many of these problems occur because each of the five 'S's' tends to be developed incrementally, and in a manner which is fragmented from the other areas of interdependent change.

Feeding in your analysis

The five 'S's' model is useful, therefore for ensuring that the key enablers and constraints are fully brought to the surface. Ideally, the five S's model should be used prior to a force field analysis to ensure that this analysis is complete. Also, it is useful in helping understand and respond to the dynamics of change, especially in the planning and control phases.

A major dilemma which is often faced in implementing strategic change is where to start an intervention — which sub-system in the 'Five S' model to begin with. For instance, if one begins with more tangible areas of change, such as systems and structures, then the advantages are felt in terms of early benefits, and change is made open and visible. However, some of the other areas of change may have longer in-built lags, such as skills and style. One might, therefore, argue that efforts in these 'softer' areas should run in parallel with or precede efforts to intervene in systems and structures. But intervening in softer areas within the five S's, first, might fall foul of lack of clarity in changes within systems and structures.

This is where 'strategy' comes in, as with a clear and detailed change strategy many of the change activities can move forward early and in parallel, creating a 'convoy' effect.

The Five 'S's' model should also highlight interdependencies between changes. This can provide valuable input to the project management of change, which is a major planning implementation and control tool (see the later section in this chapter).

The virtue of the five 'S's' is that it is simple, both pictorially and in how it represents the interaction between systems of change. It also highlights choices in where to begin and phase-in change in different areas, and also tests the robustness of the force field analysis. But, in addition to change systems analysis, the key stakeholders within the change process need to be analysed in order to draw up a truly robust force field analysis, to which we now turn.

CASE EXERCISE

For a current change issue, identify its impact on strategy, structure, skills, systems, and style. How do these elements interact with one another? Where do they suggest you begin any initiative or intervention? What do they suggest may be the potential enablers and constraining forces in progressing the change?

STAKEHOLDER ANALYSIS

Reshaping change — the impact of influence

Stakeholder analysis is our fourth change tool and should not be downplayed simply because it comes 'fourth'. In a number of cases, stakeholder analysis has been used so that it has entirely reshaped the way in which a change strategy has been communicated and moved forward through an organisation. It is also an invaluable tool for dealing with any management issue where influence is at stake.

Stakeholder analysis is the systematic identification of key stakeholders and appraisal of their influence on, and posture towards the change. It may also involve creating a strategy to reshape the influence of these or new stakeholders.

The tool is relatively simple to use, as follows:

- First, identify who you believe the key stakeholders are at any phase of the change process (the 'stakeholder brainstorm').
- Second, evaluate whether these stakeholders have high, medium or low influence on the issue in question . (You need to abstract this from their influence generally in the organisation — Piercy, 1989.)
- Third, evaluate whether at the current time they are for the change, against it, or idling in 'neutral'.

The above gives a good 'first cut' of the pattern of stakeholders. The cluster of stakeholders depicted on a stakeholder grid (see Figure 4.5) should then be assessed to see what the overall picture looks like, particularly:

- Is the change an easy bet?
- Or is it highlighting a long slog?
- Or, finally, does this seem like 'mission impossible'?

Following the first-cut analysis you should then move on to the next phase:

- First, can new stakeholders be brought into play to shift the balance, or can existing players be withdrawn in some way (or subtly distracted)?
- Second, is it possible to boost the influence of stakeholders who are currently in favour of the change?
- Third, is it possible to reduce the influence of antagonistic stakeholders?
- Fourth, can coalitions of stakeholders in favour be achieved so as to strengthen their combined influence?
- Fifth, can coalitions of stakeholders antagonistic to the change be prevented?
- Sixth, can the change itself, in appearance or in substance, be reformulated to diffuse hostility to the change?
- Seventh, are there possibilities of 'bringing on board' negative stakeholders by allowing them a role or in incorporating one or more of their prized ideas?

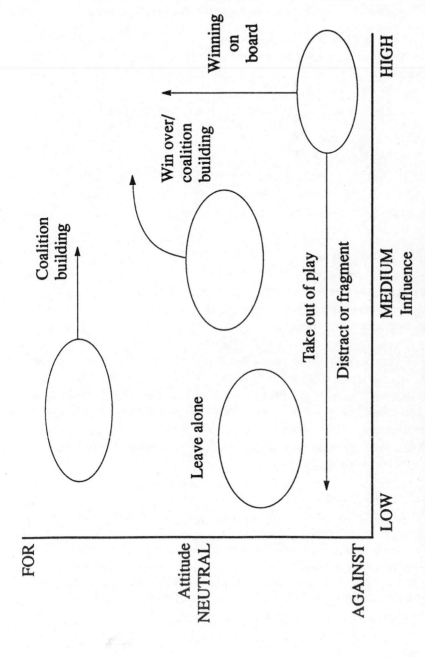

Note: This tool is based on earlier versions by Piercy (1989).

Figure 4.5 Stakeholder analysis

- Eighth, is the pattern of influence of stakeholders sufficiently hostile for the change to warrant re-definition of the change project?

Some of the strategies that can be evolved through stakeholder analysis are ones which are not immediately obvious. For example, in a strategic cost review the operations manager charged with cutting cost levels whilst sustaining competitive advantage, did not think of drawing 'on board' the new group finance director who, it was felt, might be hostile to plans for change. As it turned out, this assumption was grounded principally in fear rather than in hard evidence. The group finance director turned from being a potentially hostile antagonist to an 'influential supporter'. This example shows how this stakeholder analysis brings to the surface some of the most sticky blocks and barriers to change which the unwary can leave untouched.

Protecting the innocent

In order to use stakeholder analysis effectively you may need to set some process arrangements in place where a team project is involved. First, the analysis may be usefully done in a 'workshop' environment so as to give the analysis a 'reflective' or 'learning' feel. This helps to integrate managers' thinking on a key change issue. Also, it may be useful to devise code-words for key stakeholders in order to make the outputs from this change tool feel 'safe'. On several occasions managers have decided to adopt nicknames for the key players. The element of humour helps to diffuse the seriousness of stakeholder analysis. (For example, in my own case, 'Tony Grundy' was turned by one set of managers into a rather transparent 'Sony Grundig'.)

CASE EXERCISE

For a change issue of your choice, what is the pattern of influence and positioning of key stakeholders (for, neutral, or against)? How can this pattern be reshaped to pull the change towards its objective? (You are invited to brainstorm creative influencing strategies.)

CHANGE PROJECT MANAGEMENT

Mobilising for change

All areas of macro and most micro-level areas of change are amenable to managing as change projects. The benefits of change projects as a management process are that they:

- help managers to perform 'diagnosis' and planning of the change process more thoroughly and the definition of a clear objective for change;
- provide a vehicle for control;
- can help identify the key stakeholders in the project;
- provide clear ownership for the change;
- necessary resources are highlighted and can be mobilised in good time.

> *Change project management* is the focusing of change into one or more discrete projects to reach a pre-planned result within a specified time and cost whilst managing interdependencies with other projects and activities.

Change project management, therefore, provides essential hardware for planning and controlling change. In all three of the change cases in Part Two, project management techniques were used either explicitly or implicitly, and to good effect.

Some problems and pitfalls

Pitfalls of using project management processes include:

- The specific change is seen in isolation and unlinked to other activities or areas of change
- The process becomes weighed down with too much control bureaucracy
- Project management is not seen as fitting the organisational paradigm and may be resisted.

In the words of a leading change consultant: 'Project management is not rocket science, it is about the systematic thinking through of what you are trying to achieve, how, by whom, and when and with what result.'

Let us deal with the potential pitfalls listed above, in turn. First, project systems tend to mirror managers' natural incremental tendencies in thinking about change. This does not, however, need to be inevitable, as a project management process can be used to open up the interdependencies. Useful insights can be gained by mapping interdependencies between all change projects specifying outputs, inputs and broad time scales. Besides revealing mismatches, this will also highlight the extent to which change is being implemented in a coherent way. It may also show that the change load exceeds organisational capacity and suggest revision of change objectives to make this achievable.

Second, it is essential to avoid cumbersome bureaucracy. Few texts on project management explain how to implement this process without going over-board, with the notable exception of Andersen et al's book (1987) on *Goal-Directed Project Management*. A recipe for success is knowing when to stop: project management provides a framework but needs to be sufficiently simple so that undue time is not spent simply on maintaining reporting systems. This also needs to be linked to the communication needs of the particular change: these may change over the project's lifetime and, therefore, a fixed system would be inappropriate.

Third, where project management is seen as foreign to the paradigm, management needs to be aware that introducing it as a process is in itself a change. This suggests that change project management should be introduced in a 'pilot' or on a learning basis so that managers can get a taste of the benefits and also to minimise the effects of learning costs.

But in some situations 'the paradigm' may be completely alien and antagonistic to the project management process. This sends warning signals about organisational capability itself, as it suggests a high degree of inflexibility. Where an organisation faces ongoing and often unpredictable change, not to have access to a well-bedded-in project management process is a major competitive handicap.

The introduction of project management as a major tool for implementing change across the organisation may require changes in structure (through greater role flexibility) and also in style. In the transition period, managers may perceive the changeover to project management as generating more rather than less work in the short term. This requires careful management of expectations to ensure that managers are not rapidly switched off this invaluable tool. It also requires evaluation to show that project management is genuinely both achieving benefits and saving time.

As put by a (leading) project management consultant:

> Most of my work comes from helping rescue companies who have embarked with great enthusiasm on project management processes. They buy the latest software which splurges out lots of reports which get people into all kinds of trouble. If only people would think a little more about how project management involves a revolution in how you set about the management process. It involves a steep learning curve where tools are gradually assimilated — otherwise there is the wrong kind of big bang.

In conclusion, project management provides powerful infrastructure to the change process which enables teams to mobilise for change far more effectively and efficiently than is feasible purely within functional and hierarchical structures. To test this out, attempt the following case exercise on project managing change:

CASE EXERCISE — PROJECT MANAGEMENT

For a change initiative which you may be thinking of project managing:

- What are the key objectives of the project? Consider:
  - strategic objectives
  - operational objectives
  - organisational objectives
  - financial objectives
- To what extent do these objectives interrelate or where? Are there any inconsistencies or tensions here which need to be eliminated or managed?
- How can these objectives be communicated in a simple but clear rationale?
- What is the scope of the project — what is in it and what is outside its scope?
- How does it interrelate with other projects?
- How might it disrupt ongoing business activities and with what potential effect on performance?
- Who are the stakeholders (directly and indirectly)?
- Who will project manage it and how?
- What will the project team look like in terms of skills, its technical *and* political, multi-functional representation, and adequate seniority?

- What are the timescales and costs?
- What are the key milestones for progress?
- What resources are required and by when?
- What are the enabling and constraining forces which will impact on the project (tangible and less tangible)?
- How are these likely to change over time?
- What is the business case for the project and how will we review the net benefits less costs?

SUMMARY

This chapter described four different, but interrelated, tools for analysing and mobilising for change. These should be coupled with frameworks from previous chapters, particularly:

- From Chapter 2: the 'paradigm' tool, which examines 'how we do things around here'. This can provide important input in identifying the 'change objective' ('how do we want to do things around here in the future?') and also in identifying possible enablers and constraints (force field analysis).
- From Chapter 3: the five-stage model, which highlights how these specific power tools fit into the change process.

Amplifying the latter point, Figure 4.6 highlights which power tools can be used when in the change process.

Figure 4.6 highlights how the change tools can be used throughout the change process. Each tool enables managers to gain a valuable perspective at each phase of the change. By using more than one tool it is possible to gain a multi-perspective view of the change. This ensures that you do not miss factors which appear minor at the time, but subsequently halt the change process in its tracks.

Using the entire tool kit in this way demands some practice and perseverance. This does not mean that the tools are used slavishly, rather that they are used at the critical moments when change needs to be steered. They should not therefore intrude in 'getting on with the change'.

This brings us to the end of the first part of the book. If (as is suspected) you may have glossed over some of the exercises, it is recommended that

	Paradigm analysis	Force field analysis	Change systems	Stakeholder analysis	Change project management
Diagnosis	Setting change objectives. Input to force field analysis.	Scoping the problem. Reshaping strategy for change.	Scoping the change Highlighting inter-dependencies.	Input to force field analysis. Refining the change.	Defining the change project — inputs, process, outputs.
Planning	Defining duration of change.	Minimising effects of constraints.	Phasing interventions.	Bringing on board stakeholders.	Setting milestones & resources planning.
Implementation	Interpreting blockages.	Dealing with barriers.	Managing inter-dependencies.	Tactical management-stakeholders	Mobilising for change.
Control	Monitoring paradigm shift.	Identifying ongoing constraints.	Reshaping the change project.	Identifying new stakeholders.	Progress reporting.
Learning	Have we really changed?	Why did we succeed or fail?	Did we align the changes?	Did our intervention strategies work?	Did we meet objectives (quality, cost, time)?

Figure 4.6   Fitting all the change tools together within the change process

you go back and complete these prior to moving on to get maximum value from this guide.

For more studious readers, we now move into three major cases of change to illustrate and reinforce the lessons which have already been brought out. This is followed by Chapter 8, which brings these cases and our first four chapters together to reflect on the more general lessons from the cases.

PART TWO

LINKING VISION AND ACTION

5

CREATING A STRATEGIC VISION FOR CHANGE

INTRODUCTION

This chapter brings together a number of themes which have already been explored in this book. It begins by distilling the key lessons from the three, core cases. It then picks up the tools for implementing change in Chapters 1 to 4 and relates these to an overall framework for creating a vision for change. This is fleshed out later in this chapter through a series of questions in the form of checklists for creating a strategic vision.

LESSONS FROM LIVE CASES

The three core cases of Dowty Group's IT Division, Prudential Life Administration and ICL in Part Three will highlight a number of key lessons in creating a vision for change. Those lessons are best defined by focusing on the three elements which linked our original framework for understanding strategic change — strategy, structure and culture. These linking elements were:

- Mission;
- Leadership;
- Paradigm.

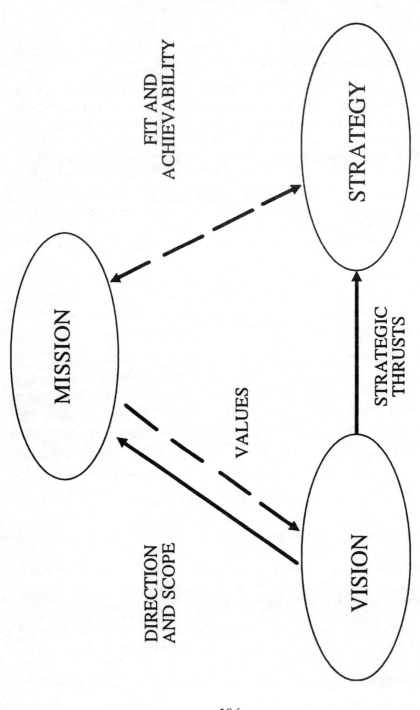

Figure 5.1   Linking mission, vision and strategy

Mission

Key points on mission (see Figure 5.1) are that:

- The 'mission' needs to be sufficiently simple so that it can be communicated without distortion. But it needs to have sufficient substance to be a meaningful guide for all in the organisation.
- The mission should build from the organisation's distinctive strengths — especially those which ultimately derive from its culture.
- The mission must not be a 'mirage' — a dream which is not feasible whatever the business strategy (whether deliberate or 'emergent').
- It should not be overly quantitative and contain fixed targets or goals which will render it fast obsolescent.
- It should expose the organisation's core values. These may be primarily aimed at, for example, 'securing shareholder value' or may be multiple and include, for instance, contributing to customer, staff and supplier development and welfare. Where values are exposed, these must truly reflect the behaviour and attitudes of all organisational levels — right up to top management.

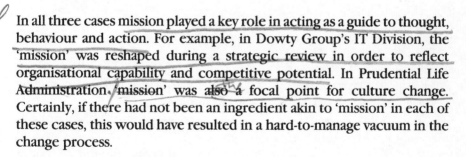

In all three cases mission played a key role in acting as a guide to thought, behaviour and action. For example, in Dowty Group's IT Division, the 'mission' was reshaped during a strategic review in order to reflect organisational capability and competitive potential. In Prudential Life Administration 'mission' was also a focal point for culture change. Certainly, if there had not been an ingredient akin to 'mission' in each of these cases, this would have resulted in a hard-to-manage vacuum in the change process.

Leadership

Key points on leadership are that:

- The leadership must be both clear and committed to the business strategy and must not hesitate or be ashamed to articulate its mission.
- Leadership must be open about tactical pressures to deviate from 'the strategy' and must be prepared to trade these off explicitly and openly rather than seek to bury the issue.
- There should be firm co-ordination by leaders of the communication

strategy with more attention being given to communicating strategic change issues effectively rather than less.

- Leaders must behave in ways consistent with desired culture and values on a day-to-day basis — momentary lapses will be magnified and rapidly publicised through the internal grapevine.
- Leaders must be prepared (where and when appropriate) to act decisively, for example in making key staff changes, but when it does this needs to be set in context — especially in terms of the strategy, likely impact on structure, and fit with culture and values.
- Good leaders are not shy and draw back from using internal or external agents of change in order to accelerate change and remove or go around barriers.

Again, as will be seen in all three cases, the quality of leadership played a decisive influence on whether the original objectives of strategic change were attained and at what cost and with what difficulty. Success depended not merely on being assertive and having total commitment to change, but also on having the staying power to achieve results and resist compromise.

Paradigm

Key points on the role of the organisational paradigm are that:

- Changes that have a significant impact on the organisational paradigm are likely to be particularly hard to implement.
- These kind of changes are likely to take much longer than originally anticipated to fully work through.
- Where an organisation has undergone rapid development or change in recent years this can lead to a diversity of sub-paradigms which are hard or perhaps impossible to align. This calls for a combination of tolerated diversity and efforts to compensate for 'different ways of doing things around here'. The concept of the 'internal customer' can be a powerful idea to help reduce barriers between sub-paradigms.
- In understanding the organisation's capability for change, the 'paradigm' may highlight where the major barriers are, especially in terms of inflexible structures and cultures and in empty organisational rituals.

Again, the 'paradigm' played a crucial role in both setting the direction for change and in helping or hindering its progress in all three cases. For instance, at Dowty Group's IT Division, paradigm shift was an issue which crystallised or emerged as the change progress progressed. At the Prudential it became a useful way of separating out 'old' behaviours from 'new'.

A FRAMEWORK FOR CREATING THE VISION

This section introduces the checklists for creating a strategic vision for change. These are structured in three main parts: environmental analysis, competitive analysis, and capability analysis. A final section to synthesise areas of linkage is also defined. These questions provide precursors to analysing a more specific change which flows on from the strategic vision. Questions concerned with the implementation of change (as opposed to setting the direction of changes) are addressed in the next chapter.

Environmental analysis deals with the external changes which may reshape the industry which an organisation is in. By 'industry' is meant the patterns of demand and supply of goods or services and of their distribution and of competition between suppliers. Environmental analysis may involve political and regulatory change, economic change, social and demographic change, technology-based and international change.

Competitive analysis, by contrast, focuses not so much on the wider factors in the industry environment but on change within the industry itself. This includes change in industry scope and barriers, shifts in competitive groupings and power and finally the effects of industry life-cycle and other dynamic factors.

Finally, *capability analysis* deals with economic and financial capability, strategic and marketing capability and organisational capability (Ulrich and Lake, 1990).

So what is new with this framework? Is this just old wine in new bottles, or do the checklists deliver a robust strategic vision faster and more easily? The answer to the first question is that little within the checklists is, of itself, strictly 'new'. Its novelty is the tight distillation of factors in just over 16 key questions. Some of these may be more pertinent than others, so any company is likely to find a core of key questions which will move a management team towards creating a strategic vision. Each question is thus supported by a number of other questions, which are there only as a checklist. In a single, one-day workshop it will only be possible to focus on a relatively small number of key questions — perhaps four or five — and on a sub-set of the supporting questions. The key questions are found in the headings — these are the essential issues on which to focus. Refer to the supporting questions from the workshop to check that you are covering all the right ground.

Not only is it important to explore the potential for industry shift from factors within the wider environment on a particular industry's competitive structure, but the environmental fit which links the external environment to organisational capability is also of interest. This highlights how an organisation is linked to its wider environment. For instance, if we assume that 'people' are one of the key sources of an organisation's competitive advantage, to sustain capability it needs to compete against other companies for the best skills — and not necessarily in the same industry.

Where an organisation is in a 'sleepy' industry, with old-fashioned ideas of hierarchical and deferential management styles, this alone will deter lively managers from coming in to revitalise the organisation.

Another issue is where the organisation may (in financial performance terms) be thriving, but this may mask an increasing gap between its own values and those of the wider business and social environment. It was considered perfectly acceptable in the 1980s for corporate entities to focus primarily (if not exclusively) on creating 'shareholder value'. However, it is just possible (although I make no predictions) that in the late 1990s and by 2000 we will have seen a seachange in value systems towards 'constrained materialism'. This may cause some companies which have espoused 'pure financial strategies' to reconsider their own value systems — otherwise they may find themselves gradually ostracised, which will, in turn, generate financial costs.

WHAT TO DO AND HOW TO DO IT

The bewildered manager who is wondering how to begin to create a 'strategic vision' should now gain assurance from what follows. The extensive checklists are simply prompts to thinking. To use the framework it is suggested that your team conducts an issue analysis for the strategic vision by asking:

- How is our wider environment changing and how does this affect where we want to be in the future?
- How are changes in competitive forces likely to affect us in the future?
- Where are we now in terms of our competitive position and organisational capability?
- What is the gap between where we are and where we want to, or need to be in the future?

These four questions are sufficient fuel to run a full one-day team workshop. The 'strategic vision' questions in this chapter provide further prompts to raise issues which may be missed at the relatively high level of the above questions.

Final case — Creating Strategic Vision in the National Health Service

The National Health Service in the UK has recently undergone major and traumatic changes. The UK government is keen to introduce concepts such as a 'market' for services, the 'patient's charter', reduced waiting times, higher quality and lower costs. Besides restructuring the role of commissioning health authorities versus providers, provider units have been rapidly transformed into 'businesses'.

One health district launched a major effort to create a strategic vision. This involved workshops with middle/senior managers to bring to the surface and test issues, before the board of the unit started the process of devising a strategic vision. Following these successful sessions, a six-hour strategic vision workshop was held with the top team of eighteen, directors and 'lead clinicians'. As had been previously anticipated by the chief executive officer, the director of human resources and by the facilitator, this group proved to be unwieldly. Despite this constraint, it was possible to make good progress towards a 'strategic vision' by asking a small number of key questions remarkably similar to the four touched on above.

The workshops produced several results: further steps were taken to firm up ownership of the 'strategic vision', and a number of small 'task forces' were set up to focus on the many implementation issues which had been identified which might frustrate realisation of 'the vision'. The top team was also slimmed down, as it was realised that it was too unwieldly a vehicle, not merely for analysis and choice, but also for steering implementation.

Once again, this exercise highlights the importance of pressing on until a satisfactory and owned vision is achieved rather than being frustrated by not having achieved, full clarity in a single attempt.

CHECKLISTS FOR CREATING A STRATEGIC VISION

These checklists are designed to enable the senior management team to create a vision of external change and internal change upon which to base a strategy. This vision needs to be defined first in terms of time horizon and business scope, although this may need to be revisited. The checklists are structured in three main areas following the suggestions of Chapter 8 along with a further section of 'synthesis' as follows:

- environmental analysis;
- competitive analysis;
- capability analysis;
- synthesis.

How these knit together to generate strategic vision is shown in Figure 5.2 on page 119.

Each of the three core areas — environmental, competitive and capability analysis — should not be taken in isolation, but should be related to each of the other two components in order to achieve a complete vision. The checklists are indebted to Porter (1985) and Ulrich and Lake (1990). Their novelty lies, however, in the fusion of ideas from many perspectives which they represent and the tightly distilled form in which they are structured.

In order to create a strategic vision it is recommended that each subsection is evaluated to see a) what the implications are for 'where you are now' (current position) versus b) 'where you want to be' (future position) and c) your broad strategies for moving from a) to b). This does not involve creation of full-blown competitive strategies and programmes for change but gives an overview sufficiently clear to guide more detailed strategy definition.

CREATING A STRATEGIC VISION FOR CHANGE

ENVIRONMENTAL ANALYSIS

Key questions are structured as follows:

- political and regulatory change;
- economic change;
- social and demographic change;
- technology change;
- international change.

How may political and regulatory change impact on your strategy?

- What new political interventions are likely, either from an existing or new government, which might significantly affect the industry?
- Is it likely that de-regulation will substantially reshape the industry and, if so, over what period?
- What other regulatory changes (legal, environmental, safety etc) may shift 'the rules of the game' for your business?
- What is the impact of moves towards standards-setting on product development and maintaining existing business?

How may economic change impact on your strategy?

- How is the economic cycle likely to affect the way in which strategic change can be managed?
- To what extent has the economic cycle obscured more fundamental change in external markets (for instance, customers may have become permanently more value-conscious following a recession)?
- How is economic change likely to be affected by political and regulatory change and what is the specific impact on your industry likely to be?
- How is the longer-term development of your market-place influenced by changes in patterns of demand at a macro-economic level? Have these been reflected in your business strategy?

How may social and demographic change impact on your strategy?

- What social trends exist which may reshape the values and behaviours of consumers, and, thus, how demand is met in your industry?

- What social trends exist which may reshape the way in which people do business in the industry?
- Does your strategy reflect changes in demographic patterns, for instance in the number of people in particular age groups, their purchasing power and changing life styles?
- What are the specific demographic trends in the geographic area(s) where your business has greatest concentration?

How will technological change impact on your strategy?

- What new or emerging technologies may reshape your industry?
- Who will be the leading players in exploiting this technology (not only in the UK, but in Europe and globally)?
- Will the transformation be slow and incremental or will it be more sudden and revolutionary?
- Will the greatest impact of technology be through:
  — raising entry barriers?
  — threat of substitutes?
  — breaking down industry barriers?
  — altering the relative power of suppliers and buyers?
  — forcing industry regroupings or alliances?
  — undermining or proliferating possibilities for differentiation?
  — creating new possibilities for cost leadership?

How will international change impact on your strategy?

- How is your industry likely to be affected by any move (post 1992) towards a 'Single European Market'?
- To what extent is your industry vulnerable to competition from Eastern sources and how is this likely to manifest itself over the longer-term (ie the next 3-10 years)?
- Do changes in Eastern Europe (and the former Soviet Union) represent opportunities or threats, and if so, over what time scale?
- What effect might international movements to improve or protect the global environment have on your industry?
- Will your industry become increasingly susceptible to cross-border acquisitions and alliances?
- How will change in international financial markets inhibit or facilitate industry development?

COMPETITIVE ANALYSIS

Key questions are structured as follows:

- scope of the industry and barriers;
- competitive groupings and power;
- industry life-cycle and dynamics.

How is the industry's scope and its barriers changing?

- What are the traditional boundaries of the industry and how are these changing?
- What is the relationship between this industry and other adjacent industries, either closer to the end-consumer or further away from the end-consumer?
- What entry barriers exist and how are these changing as a result of new technology, cost economies, changes in definition of geographical markets, etc?
- What 'exit' barriers exist and how are these amplified by industry psychology in seeking to 'stay in the game'? How are these barriers changing?
- What activities in the industry add most value and who has the tightest grip over these activities and how? What trends exist that reflect changes in how value is added?

What are the main competitive groupings and how is power distributed

- What is the extent of competitive rivalry in the industry and how is it dependent upon changes in groupings of key players?
- How powerful are buyers relative to the company and the main competitors?
- How powerful are suppliers relative to the company and its main competitors?
- How important are substitutes either from other types of product or service or from internal substitutes from customers 'doing it themselves'?
- How are all these forces likely to interact with one another and shift the focus of power in the future?

- How is the pattern of any increasing competitive activity likely to impact on future profit?
- Does this suggest possible ways of intervening to improve the industry structure without adverse effects?

How will industry life-cycle and dynamics affect the business?

- How is your industry affected by its life-cycle particularly in virtue of its being:
  — emergent?
  — high growth?
  — maturing?
  — mature?
  — in decline?
  — in between one of these stages?
- More specifically, what key changes are about to be seen in terms of:
  — possibilities for differentiation?
  — through having a low cost base and lower prices than the competition?
  — the importance of meeting or beating industry standards for quality?
  — industry restructuring as profitable opportunities decline in a fragmented, competitive market place?
- What does this suggest for defining your critical success factors in terms of organisational capability?

CAPABILITY ANALYSIS

The main ingredients of capability analysis (Ulrich and Lake, 1990) are:

- economic and financial capability;
- strategic and marketing capability;
- technological capability;
- organisational capability.

What is our current economic and financial capability?

- Do we have the financial resources and position necessary to support the scale of changes envisaged?

- Where this assumes the backing of 'group' or external stakeholders, has this support been agreed and will it be sustained?
- Will this support be undermined by changes in the economic and competitive environment?
- Do we have the necessary financial skills to ensure that the benefits of pursuing a given change strategy are not merely evaluated but also harvested and measured?

What is our current strategic and marketing capability?

- Do we have a clear enough vision of the scope of our business, its fit with the environment, of our sustainable competitive advantage and of the key changes needed in order to implement our strategy?
- Is this shared with *all* key managers involved in making or implementing decisions which shape the strategy?
- Is this vision based on realistic and 'outside-in' views of our competitive strengths and weaknesses (for example, through customer or competitor analysis or by bench-marking)?
- Does our culture reflect a clear understanding of market and customer needs throughout the organisation or is it one which is introverted and lacks innovation?
- Are specific parts of the organisation (for example, the finance function or the sales force or operations management) tactically orientated, or is its mind-set geared to achieving a longer-term strategy?
- Does our product/market mix line up neatly behind a small number of strategic thrusts or are these fragmented, cluttered and complex (if not confused)?
- Do we have a coherent strategy for exploiting indirect channels to market which does not generate major conflict with direct sales strategy?
- What is the calibre of our direct salesforce (compared to the competition)?

What is our current technological capability?

- How good are we at exploiting existing and new technologies for commercial benefit?

- How effective are we in exploiting synergies between areas of know-how irrespective of where it exists in the organisation?
- How good are we at tapping into the technology base of our suppliers?
- Is our technology (and competitive) base actually weakened or strengthened by strategic alliances and over what time scales?
- Do we provide sufficient investment resource to develop our technology capability? Is it applied in those most critical areas which will add most value over the long term?

What is our current organisational capability?

- Is our organisation responsive to the external environment in terms of:
  — being genuinely flexible to customer need?
  — responding quickly to short-term change?
  — being willing to contemplate making major changes where these are vital?
- Do managers and staff have a genuinely outward facing culture and reflect this in regular visits to customers, suppliers and other world-class companies or are they introverted?
- Does our capacity for change match the change imperatives which the organisation faces?
- Is our 'leadership' generally 'world-class' or is it average or mediocre?
- Does the management process create cohesion or does it generate fragmentation, a bias towards undue short-term behaviour and unnecessary politicking?
- Do we work effectively (at *all* levels) as teams?
- Are we genuinely 'open' in dealing with problems (whether small or large)?
- Are we able to communicate the 'strategic vision' effectively and to all appropriate levels?
- Are middle and senior managers receptive to working in flat and flexible structures or do they yearn after hierarchy?
- Do we have a ready supply of young 'new blood' to revitalise the organisation.
- Are top management consistent in practising what they preach?
- Is 'quality' as a concept firmly rooted in the organisation as a way of life?

- Is there a mind-set of doing things because they 'add value' or because 'we like doing these things around here'?
- Has the company an internationally-facing culture or one which is parochial?

SYNTHESIS

This short section brings together the three areas of analysis covered in the previous questions. These interrelate:

- environmental and competitive conditions;
- competitive and capability analysis;
- environmental and capability analysis;
- the strategic vision itself.

How might the wider environment and the competitive conditions of the industry interact?

Is the industry itself facing major loss of profitability because of changes in the wider environment?
- How might the balance of competitive forces be shaped by:
  — political and regulating factors?
  — economic change?
  — social and demographic change?
  — technology change?
  — international change?

How will our competitive position impact on organisational capability and vice versa?

- Is the organisation's own view of its strengths and weaknesses tested against its competitors and customers and are key lessons drawn from this?
- Is this testing made at a detailed level as part of operational benchmarking?
- Is this fed back directly into organisational learning, decision-making and change?

How may environmental change interact with organisational capability?

- Is the structure and culture of the organisation in tune with the wider business environment?
- Does its strategic vision not only seek fit within its wider environment, but also seek ways in which that environment can be reshaped to be favourable to the organisation?
- To what extent does technological capability lead or lag 'best world practices'?
- How can the external environment be used to amplify internal change, eg through corporate advertising or through publicising internal change?

Is the strategic vision complete?

Does the strategic vision:

- Give a broad idea of how the organisation will compete?
- Indicate how it fits within its wider environment?
- Define its core sources of organisational capability, particularly those which it believes are distinctive?
- Feel as if it is exciting and stretching without appearing unrealistic and unachievable?

To conclude, it would be ideal to achieve a reasonably complete and robust account of a strategic vision which answered most of the key questions and addressed the checklist. It is likely, however, that any management team would require at least two to three days of workshops to cover a part of this ground. An alternative approach is to pick off a few key issues at a time and begin to build up a strategic vision over a longer period. This may be more feasible in practical terms, but may not give a sufficient overview if the environment is undergoing major change.

Vision building of this kind provides a feed-in to more detailed strategic planning. It may also provide the ground from which to define a mission statement, which is a higher level than the picture painted within the strategic vision. Figure 5.1 (see page 105) highlights how vision, mission and strategy interrelated with strategic vision being used to define both mission and strategy, with ongoing cross-checks between mission and strategy for achievability and consistency.

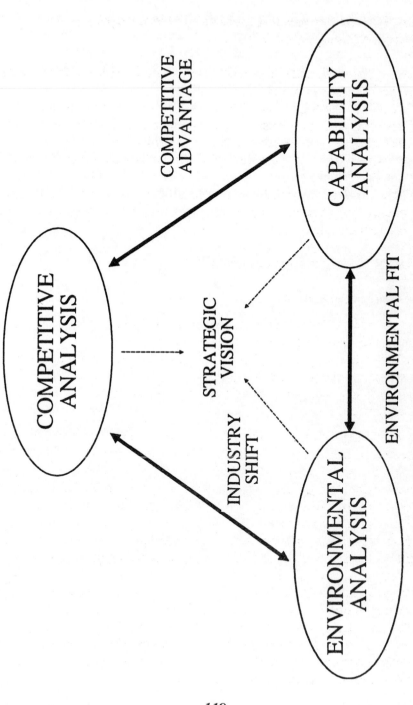

Figure 5.2   Creating a strategic vision

The model of strategic planning which strives to get a strategic vision 'right' at periodic intervals is doomed (at least in most environments) to failure. In its place, strategic thinking can help cover main issues. This involves ongoing strategic thinking which deals with issues in rotation. As much as 80 per cent of the most important issues can thus be covered with about 20 per cent of the effort required to cover all of the issues, satisfying the Pareto principle.

The strategic vision questions aim to tease out and evaluate issues and to identify patterns rather than programmes for action. The programmes themselves should become clear once the implementation plans — addressed in the next chapter — are set in place.

6

CHECKLISTS FOR IMPLEMENTING STRATEGIC CHANGE

INTRODUCTION

These checklists are designed to provide managers with a lasting guide to helping them manage change on a day-to-day basis. This applies at the organisational level, at the level of more specific areas of change and also within managers' individual roles. The checklists are structured in four key phases as follows:

- understanding the context of managing change, especially to reflect the 'macro-' or high-level forces impacting on change within the strategic vision (see Chapter 5);
- managing the process, including diagnosis, planning, implementation, control, learning;
- analysing content issues, externally, internally and cross-functionally;
- managing specific change applications , including, for example, restructuring, quality, culture change, acquisitions and managing individual role transitions.

Because the management of people permeates the checklists, a separate section to deal with 'people' is not provided.

UNDERSTANDING THE MACRO CONTEXT OF CHANGE

1. Does the proposed change impact (directly or indirectly) on strategy, structure, culture or on a mix of these key ingredients of strategic change?

2. Do we propose to manage it as if all three (or two) elements are affected by macro-level change or in relative isolation (and if the latter, then why)?

3. Does the pace and degree of internal change genuinely match the pace of change in the external business environment where this is a key driver of internal change?

4. Is there appropriate leadership to steer the change through?

5. Does the 'mission' adequately reflect a) a realistic strategy for the business in enabling it to compete, b) the underlying values implicit in corporate culture?

6. Does the proposed change fit with the organisational paradigm or seek to achieve a 'paradigm shift'?

7. Is any change intervention of sufficient critical mass and well focused enough to achieve a quantum shift in the paradigm?

8. How central is this change intervention positioned in the organisation and what ongoing attention (both symbolic and real) is top management prepared to give it?

MANAGING THE PROCESS

The five key phases of managing change are:

- diagnosis;
- planning;
- implementation;
- control;
- learning.

Diagnosis

1. Have we identified the real nature of the 'change problem' or 'opportunity'?

2. Have we diagnosed 'where we currently are'?

3. Is the 'change objective' clearly specified in terms of where we want to be and with what tangible benefits and by when?

4. How wide is the 'change gap' between where we are now and where we need to be, and how does this stack up against preconceived ideas of how long and difficult the change process will be?

5. What are the key enabling and constraining factors within both the change and its context which will influence progress towards meeting the change objectives?

6. Have these 'key change forces' picked up both tangible and less tangible factors as they now are (ie not in terms of an 'ideal') in the change process, for example:
   — leadership;
   — communication;
   — skills;
   — key stakeholders;
   — readiness for change;
   — culture and style;
   — systems;
   — adequacy of resources;
   — timescales;
   — clarity of change plans.

7. Do any of these forces identify possible 'stoppers'?

8. What is the overall 'balance' of forces — do these show the change as being 'manageable', 'very difficult' or as 'mission impossible'?

9. Has the strategy for change now been reshaped in the light of the force field analysis?

10. Has a stakeholder analysis been performed in order to ensure a) the force field analysis is complete, and b) to evolve influencing strategies to help mobilise commitment to change?

Planning

1. Has the overall 'objective for change' (per the 'diagnosis' phase) been refined into a small number (less than five) of more detailed and specific change objectives?

2. Are these objectives supported by key change milestones which specify:
   a) phases of the change process;

b) clear outputs and outcomes of each phase;

c) who is responsible for achieving these milestones?

3. Has a network of appropriately resourced activities been drawn up to support the achievement of these milestones?

4. Has the change project been thoroughly evaluated in terms of tangible and less tangible benefits and costs and who are these 'owned' by in the organisation?

5. What key risks and uncertainties have been identified? Does this include interdependencies with other areas of change and possible changes in management intent?

6. Have the initial force field analysis and stakeholder analysis been updated for further changes since the diagnosis phase?

7. Has an appropriate and competent leader of the change been appointed and does he have a change project team with adequate skills and an appropriate style to ensure smooth implementation?

8. Has the change been suitably communicated in a skilfully targeted and timed way to *all* those playing a central role in the change *and* those indirectly affected by the change?

9. Do business plans adequately reflect any unavoidable drop in performance due to the inherent problems of managing a particularly difficult transition?

10. Is there an explicit business case for any major change?

Implementation

1. Where key milestones are not being met does this suggest that:
   — the 'problem' has not been properly defined in the first place;
   — the constraints are more severe than expected or new and unforeseen constraints surface;
   — the communication strategy did not work;
   — there is a problem of leadership or skills, or both;
   — the capability to digest change is less than was previously thought;
   — the change process requires more resource than first thought, or has been delayed or starved of resource;
   — new (antagonistic) stakeholders have emerged or support from once favourable stakeholders has ebbed away?

2. Does the above suggest that the overall change strategy needs to be revisited?

3. How can action plans now be tailored to accelerate progress or remove bottlenecks?
4. What new contingencies and risks have emerged and how might action plans be strengthened to deal with these?

Control

1. Are the milestones of the change project being met in terms of:
   — tangible benefits;
   — less tangible benefits;
   — tangible costs;
   — less tangible costs;
   — timings?
2. How effectively has the change process been implemented relative to:
   — past experience within the business area;
   — past experience of business areas elsewhere in the organisation;
   — other organisations undertaking similar change?
3. Have change management processes been applied consistently throughout the change project, including:
   — monitoring of enablers for and constraints to change and regular stakeholder analysis;
   — project management systems for planning, control and feedback?

Learning

1. Did the change actually meet its key objectives and if not, why not?
2. What should we now do, therefore, to secure the intended benefits of the change?
3. How might we influence key stakeholders to commit to any further necessary or appropriate change?
4. What lessons can now be drawn about:
   — how we diagnose, plan, implement and control change generally;
   — our overall capacity for and capability to implement change?
5. How can we disseminate these 'learning lessons' in an open way, and without embarrassment?

ANALYSIS OF CONTENT ISSUES

1. Does the change involve several departments across the organisation and if so how does this impact on how change is managed?

2. To what extent does it involve external parties and stakeholders including customers, suppliers, regulatory authorities etc — have they been brought on board with the change?

3. Is the change seen as a 'quick fix' (less than six months), a 'medium-term campaign' (between six and 18 months) or a 'long campaign' (between 18 months and five years) and is this timescale realistic?

4. Is this change resource-intensive in terms of internal technical skills, external skills or management time and will this be forthcoming?

5. What is the critically perceived degree of difficulty of change:
   — technically;
   — politically;
   and is this fully reflected in the change strategy?

6. Does the change involve cross-border management and linguistic and cultural differences and, if so, how will these be managed?

7. Is the change amenable to bench-marking? If not, how is it proposed to keep an objective track of benefits yielded and on the effectiveness of the change process?

8. Has an analysis of 'key change issues' showing key interrelationships between these issues been completed?

9. Have *all* the relevant content issues been surfaced, for example using:
   — force field analysis;
   — stakeholder analysis;
   — analysing the systems of change (strategy, structure, culture and style, people and skills, systems)?

10. Have the 'soft' and less tangible issues been given sufficient emphasis in analysing the change or does it feel as if managers want to short-cut and thereby short circuit the steps of change required?

SPECIFIC CHANGE APPLICATIONS

Introduction

A number of common applications come up regularly as key problems facing managers in the 1990s. These include:

- strategic and financial planning;
- re-structuring;
- change in specific roles and style;
- quality management;
- culture change;
- information systems;
- performance management/rewards systems;
- management development;
- organisational communication;
- managing individual role transition;
- acquisition integration;
- management buy-outs.

These are now dealt with individually in some depth.

Strategic and financial planning

1. Does the 'strategic' plan genuinely take into account the impact of external change?
2. Does it involve specific measurement of competitive advantage or disadvantage in terms of value added (and at what cost) to target customers *vis-à-vis* key competitors?
3. Is it consistent with 'mission' and is this 'mission' credible given the risk and uncertainties in achieving strategic goals?
4. Is financial appraisal used to evaluate the economic value of business strategies (ie in cash flow terms — not just 'reported' earnings projections) or are these strategies left untested in terms of shareholder value?
5. Is the strategy feasible given current financial constraints, and do these 'constraints' need testing themselves?
6. Does the strategic plan reflect the organisational and operational capability (strengths and weaknesses) of the business — can we excel in what we propose?

7. Are there clear strategic and financial milestones for success which link to quarterly or bi-annual business performance assessment?
8. Is the 'strategic plan' communicated in appropriate detail to sufficient relevant levels of management and staff responsible for implementation?
9. Is there adequate scope for 'emergent strategies' to develop within the overall strategic and financial framework — ie in-built provision for innovation and exploitation of hard-to-foresee opportunity?
10. Are adequate change mechanisms set in place to implement the strategy (for example, change project teams, off-site review workshops, rewards for actions to implement change etc)?

Restructuring

1. Is the rationale for the restructuring fully thought through and does this reflect not merely current needs but anticipate pending changes in the business?
2. Is there a history of frequent re-structuring which results in a permanent (and unnecessary) state of instability in the organisation?
3. Has the restructuring put managers into 'artificial' positions without genuine business benefits which are patently transparent and which will aggravate organisational ambiguity?
4. Are new appointees genuinely capable of being effective in their roles given their skills, their style, and also the degree of team-working within the organisation?
5. Has the restructuring been communicated in such a way to lay bare the business-led reasons for the restructuring?
6. What is the timing of announcement of restructuring — has it been deliberately timed so as to prevent reflection and debate and thereby result in simmering resentment?

Change in specific roles and style

1. Has the change been thoroughly thought through in terms of:
   — tangible benefits and costs;
   — less tangible benefits and costs;
   — risks to the business?
2. Have all the knock-on effects of the change been thought through (for instance, on the bosses and subordinates of those whose roles

have changed — not only in terms of the content of responsibilities but also in terms of style)?

3. By what method have staff been chosen to be appointed or re-appointed to positions (for example, have they gone through a thorough and recent assessment of their competences)?

Quality management

1. How does the 'quality management' initiative link in with the organisation's underlying paradigm (especially in its controls, routines, rituals and overall culture)?

2. Is the organisation (and particularly senior management) prepared for a 'long haul' on quality?

3. Is the focus of quality management mainly internal or is it inextricably linked with competitive strategy?

4. Does this focus flow through to external bench-marking of external value delivered to customers and also to bench-marking of key internal processes?

5. Have expectations of managers been set appropriately from the outset during all communication to prevent 'early cynicism'?

6. Are top management prepared to mirror quality in their own behaviour and style?

7. Which (specific) senior managers are *least* likely to behave in ways which show an active 'enthusiasm for quality'?

8. Is 'quality management' made equally applicable to major management processes (eg strategic planning, performance review and individual appraisals) as well as to more specific 'operational' issues?

9. Has it been generally accepted in the organisation that 'quality management' involves a major (and strategic) change or is it seen merely as a 'good initiative' to be doing?

10. Is there a balance between the measurement and control of performance (which quality management may imply) versus 'trust' and 'empowerment' at the individual and team level as part of a 'quality culture'?

11. Is the emphasis on quality in danger of becoming a new 'ritual' without regard for which aspects of quality are of greatest strategic value?

12. Is there an appropriate balance of effort between efforts to rectify

quality disadvantage versus efforts to achieve a distinctive advantage through quality?

Culture change

1. What is the fundamental reason for launching an attempt to manage 'culture change' — is it:
   — to get rid of 'bureaucracy';
   — to reduce complexity and cost;
   — to focus on 'the customer';
   — to remedy competitive disadvantage, or
   — to amplify the power base of a new leader?
2. Is this linked to tangible areas of change such as re-structuring, role re-definition, bringing in 'new blood', physical re-location to a new site, or to a change in ownership or status of the business? If not, how is it proposed to make the change happen without making changes of a tangible nature?
3. Has the scope of the change been fully addressed (for instance, does it cover head office, business units, international businesses — does it also penetrate a number of levels of management and operational staff)?
4. How central is 'culture change' positioned in the organisation with visible and ongoing backing of top management?
5. How will culture change effects (positive and negative) be monitored?
6. How will management track the value of culture change through tangible and less tangible impact on performance?
7. How sustainable will efforts to change the culture be — for 1, 3, 4 or more years (and at what cost)?
8. How will 'new stories' within the 'emerging paradigm' be identified and broadcast?
9. Will the culture change have tangible bite — will we be prepared to remove or sideline major antagonists?
10. How will we address the problem of 'decoy behaviour' (or behaviour paying merely lip-service to change)?

Information systems

1. Are attempts to change information systems part of an overall

information strategy which is, in turn, linked to both business strategy and intended organisational change?

2. How have the cost/benefits of change been evaluated in terms of both internal and external benefits and costs, including:
   — customer value;
   — access to markets;
   — customer 'lock-in';
   — improving responsiveness;
   — operational efficiency and capacity?

3. Are changes in information systems seen as a) primarily of a technical issue, versus b) as also generating important and more difficult people-related and political issues?

4. Who are the key stakeholders: a) of the end outputs of information systems, and b) as agents within the change process itself?

5. Is there a risk of overrun against required timescales which might result in an expensive and disruptive 'crash programme' or a dilution of project benefits?

Performance management/rewards systems

1. How are 'performance management' systems linked to strategic plans, budgets, reward systems and employee recognition?

2. How complete in scope are these systems — where these only cover part of the organisation are there plans to roll this out and are these plans well-communicated?

3. Have proposed changes in rewards systems (for example, amending company car schemes) been fully thought through in terms of their symbolic importance in the organisation?

4. Is there an appropriate balance between rewards systems versus recognition efforts to provide genuine and sustainable increases in motivation?

5. Are staff punished for making mistakes or is this seen positively as part of a 'learning process' (within limits which the business can tolerate)?

6. To what extent are staff rewarded and recognised for being proactive in moving change forward?

7. Does the converse apply if they have been negative or lethargic in managing change?

Management development

1. Is management development seen as being outside the scope of implementing strategic change, peripheral to this or alternatively as central to the change management process?
2. Where management development is targeted as a catalyst for change in the organisation:
   — Has this been centrally positioned and actively championed by top management?
   — Do development programmes help managers to understand the external and internal needs for change and translate this into concrete learning through work on live, strategic change issues?
   — Is there a channel to enable learning outputs to be fed back into the live decision-making and change process?
   — Does this provide a sufficient critical mass (in terms of complete coverage of specific business unit teams) to achieve sustainable shift in perspectives and behaviour?
   — Do these programmes deal also with the individual's own role issues in managing change and also his style as change agent?
3. Are management development efforts aligned with:
   — strategic planning and budgetary timetables (to provide both input and output to live decision processes);
   — quality management, culture change and customer care initiatives;
   — underlying plans to develop both individual and also organisational capability?

Organisational communication

1. Are efforts to improve communication primarily focused on 'sending messages down the line' or on 'two-way listening'?
2. Are communication efforts overtly formal, routine, ritualistic, and predictable — thereby dulling the force of any message?
3. Are the key signals relayed in a reasonably simple (but not in a simplistic form) — for example, having a one- or two-page rule for memos — or are they clouded in detail and ambiguity?
4. Are these key signals consistent with central themes of the mission, values and strategy of the organisation?
5. Are top managers prepared to repeat and constantly reinforce these

themes in order to provide a clear direction and framework for all actions?

6. Do top managers walk about the organisation and listen to staff, to customers and suppliers, rather than retreating into their own territorial power zones within a bureaucracy?

Managing individual role transition

1. To what extent is your new role clearly defined or is this, in many respects, ambiguous?
2. In the latter case, do you see this as an opportunity to re-shape your new role or are you in danger of 'freezing' due to uncertainty?
3. Does your new job involve a quantum change in scope or a major shift in style? (If so, it is likely that you will experience a significant drop in both performance and self-esteem during the transition).
4. Are there any 'friendly sources' of support which you can draw upon during the most difficult period of transition both within and outside the business?
5. Have you quickly identified and prioritised the key issues which need resolving during the first few months of your activity and also those which demand longer-term attention?
6. Based on the analysis (per 5), what are the critical success factors which will help you through the transition period?
7. How will you secure cohesion of your own team and their loyal support through a two-way dialogue on what they need, what you need and how both of these needs can be met?

Acquisition integration

1. What key synergies are anticipated to be harvested through the acquisition?
2. What changes are required in order to achieve these synergies — to products, services, operations, systems and processes, structures and people?
3. Who are the key people who are essential both to protect and develop the business?
4. How can they be convinced that it is worth backing the organisation following this period of pronounced uncertainty associated with the acquisition, for example through:

- selling the benefits of the acquisition in terms of future opportunity for their own development and reward;
- providing them with a clear role in the change venture;
- spelling out openly the criteria for success and failure;
- protecting their self-respect through active incorporation of 'core best practices' into a new paradigm;
- having a clear and well communicated strategy for steering change?

5. Is it planned to announce changes in leadership and structure quickly as opposed to playing a 'wait-and-see' game with the result of mounting uncertainty?

6. Will changes in systems and control routines be handled with delicacy, sensitivity and sensible timescales set to make changes? Where systems and control changes are required from 'day one' are there arrangements to support this externally?

7. How will the issue of 'culture change' be handled, especially where it is intended to integrate a large part of operations? Does this reflect pre-acquisition diagnosis of they key differences in culture between both organisations?

8. How will learning about the acquisition be secured in terms both of 'what we have got for our money' (both internal and external capability) and also on the effectiveness of integration process?

Management buy-outs

1. What are the main objectives of the buy-out and to what extent are these shared by key management stakeholders, for instance:
    - freedom from head office dictat;
    - the possibility of making a significant capital gain;
    - protection of job security;
    - challenge of developing the business into new areas;
    - opportunity to renew the management team?

2. Has the proposed management team the ability and balance to produce a quantum improvement in business performance or does it smack of 'more of the same'?

3. What tangible changes will be made to support the symbolic event of the buy-out — for example, changing the company name, relocating premises, throwing out all the old stationery, re-organising managers' old office layout, removing unnecessary status symbols?

4. Is there a robust strategy for improving the competitive position of the business or are the buy-out plans mainly aimed at producing 'the right set of numbers' to please venture capitalists?
5. Has the buy-out team got clear milestones for progress which are achievable but stretching?
6. How is it intended to deal with complaints from stakeholders who might complain that — 'I thought we would have a better, easier life as a result of the buy-out — not an early grave'?
7. How will the issue of an 'exit route' to sell the business on (where this is applicable) be managed by the management team throughout the lifetime of the buy-out?

PART THREE

ACCELERATING THE PROCESS

7

STRATEGIC-LED CHANGE WITHIN THE DOWTY GROUP

This chapter describes a case history of strategy-led change within a major division of Dowty plc. At Dowty Communications Ltd, a datacommunications company, the management team used strategic planning to generate and channel strategic change. Academics and practitioners alike can learn many lessons from this example of strategic planning and change in action.

INTRODUCTION

From the late 1960s through to the early to mid-1980s, strategic planning was heralded as the visionary process through which senior management might steer their business through increasing turbulence. Like a light-house, strategic planning was supposed to guide managers away from strategic folly. For example, planning was seen as helping managers avoid inappropriate diversification, from investing in dying businesses (Boston Consulting Group), to provide scenarios against which strategic decisions could be made, and, above all, to focus managers' operational decision-taking to exploit its competitive advantage (Porter, 1985).

In the early 1990s we see a deepening scepticism of the need for, and indeed the very wisdom of indulging in, strategic planning. Like the story about the messenger who got shot because his news was 'inappropriate', strategic planning is in danger of becoming the punch-bag of dissatisfied managers and academics alike because it has either not been properly understood or applied ineffectively.

For illustration, if we take a sample of the academic critique we find that:

- Strategies have a tendency to emerge through an often haphazard but discernible 'pattern' in a stream of decisions (Mintzberg, 1978) rather than within an all- embracing strategic planning framework.
- This process is usually an 'incremental' rather than a 'holistic' one (Quinn, 1980).
- Strategic planning, which becomes narrowly owned by a 'planning department' becomes sterile.
- The transformation of strategic planning into a more widely shared 'strategic management vision' is extremely rare, difficult to attain and requires many years of sustained effort to achieve (Goold and Quinn, 1990).
- Even when a strategic vision is attained, the barriers to action and change are often either not addressed or change is not mobilised effectively (Stonich, 1982; Johnson, 1988; Piercy, 1989).
- Even assuming that strategic change is mobilised, it is rare to find explicit and sufficient measures of strategic process (or 'strategic controls') set in place and monitored by management (Goold and Quinn, 1990).

With all this apparently going against strategic planning it is perhaps surprising that there are so many 'strategic planning' textbooks in every business bookshop and business school. These are highly prescriptive, extol the virtues of strategic planning, but devote far less space to the pitfalls and particularly the importance of management learning and links to strategic change.

This chapter aims to redress this imbalance. It contains a story about strategic planning which highlights the practical difficulties of putting it into action and links these difficulties back to academic theory. It describes a bold attempt within the division of a major UK group (Dowty plc) to use strategic planning to drive strategic change. This story is told through a case history which involves the management team using strategic planning as a vehicle for organisational learning and change.

The case history tells how strategic planning began as an attempt to understand the business. It then moves from this 'understanding' paradigm into a 'change' paradigm through recognising that a period of internal flux was required in order to re-match the organisation with its environment. I argue that strategic planning often fails, not because its tools are faulty but because it is not seen by managers as an essential part of the strategic change process.

The case history is structured as follows:

- context of the strategic plan, learning and change process;
- planning and learning — analysis;
- planning and learning — choice;
- implementation and control of change;
- conclusions.

CONTEXT

From late 1989 through to early 1991, a major part of the IT division of Dowty plc set about transforming its approach to decision-making and business control through a strategic planning process. Early on (in 1989) this initiative was not seen specifically as part of a strategic change process, nor was it explicitly recognised by the management team as a learning exercise — but by 1990 this had been realised. It was also essentially a top-down exercise.

Earlier on, in the late 1980s, Dowty Group had acquired this major, independent datacomms company which was then called CASE Communications (CASE). CASE had been a high-growth company during the early 1980s with a highly entrepreneurial management style. In the mid-1980s, CASE had embarked on various overseas ventures which did not prove successful, and a resultant dip in financial performance made CASE (then an independent plc) vulnerable to takeover.

Prior to its acquisition by Dowty, CASE had made several attempts at longer-term planning. Although these attempts had given significant thought to understanding the external environment and to considering the longer-term options, these plans were not implemented. With hindsight it seemed that this lack of implementation was due to how they had been implanted into the management process and their fit with underlying management style and culture, rather than their inherent strategic logic.

Following Dowty's acquisition of CASE, a new managing director was brought in from outside Dowty group from the information technology industry.

In late 1989, the management team escaped from their Watford site to a country retreat in order to identify a 'mission and top-down goals' for the organisation. At this meeting, a mission was agreed which fitted both the corporate mission of Dowty Group ('to be a preferred partner'). It also stated the nature of the business which Dowty Communications (as it was now re-named) would be in and its competitive scope which was to be 'international'.

This mission was also established in parallel with a check that the team believed that their long-term goals for profitable growth were consistent with Dowty Group's aspirations and requirements.

Like many strategic planning exercises, this initiative had been started with 'mission and goals', as is suggested by prescriptive theory. The danger of this approach is that top-down formulation never meshes with what is either feasible or optimal as a bottom-up basis. This needs to be identified with particular reference to the industry structure and its attractiveness and also the business' competitive position (Porter, 1985).

Following the 1989 'mission and top-down goals' workshop, the new managing director sought to:

- Improve financial controls and budgetary culture throughout the organisation. A tough, new financial director was appointed.
- Strengthen the management team through the appointment of a technology director, a director of international business, a director of business development and the internal promotion of a new, young, personnel director.
- Identify how the business could restore its past track record of profitable growth by determining where it would focus its efforts — in product, market, channel and infrastructure development, which implied the evaluation of a 'strategic plan'.

In early 1990, the enlarged top team took the next step on the strategic planning road. Assisted by a firm of consultants, who were specialists in strategic planning and who used planning techniques developed in a much more disciplined (military) environment, they held a further workshop which was aimed at preparing the way for a strategic plan. This included:

- Brainstorming a SWOT analysis (which produced a very extensive set of issues).
- Some basic 'gap analysis' which suggested that the business' top-

down goals could be met within the existing product and technology scope — the path to growth being more attractive and less risky through market development.

- Initial work on the objectives of the individual directors which would enable them to crystallise their operational responsibilities within the new structure.

The consultants' decision process was very highly structured and was implicitly a team-building event. However, progress (especially on initial objectives) was disappointingly slow. The rigidities of the planning process also appeared to constrain rather than facilitate the learning of the top team.

At the end of this second effort the initiative was put aside for several weeks while a way of moving around the impasse was sought off-line by the managing director, the director of business development and the external facilitators.

On reflection, many of the problems experienced during this early stage — when the strategic planning process was, in effect, still taxi-ing on the runway — were understandable. The management team were involved in a complex learning process (Argyris' (1977) 'double-loop learning') which they found particularly difficult as a newly formed team now operating in a new situation (post acquisition by Dowty) and on a novel and difficult task (strategic planning).

The external facilitators brought with them a process which had previously worked well in other environments. They, too, were learning about how and why their highly structured process did not seem to be working particularly well in what had evidently been a less-structured, entrepreneurial and individual culture. By this stage however, the impasse that had occurred with the top-down approach looked irretrievable.

By coincidence, about this time another consultant was asked by the newly appointed personnel director to run a 'Strategic Workshop' for a number of newly appointed general managers and their new sales director. During this workshop an exercise was run based on understanding Gluck's (1982) four phases of the evolution of planning and diagnosing CASE's own mode of planning, namely:

- annual budgeting — phase 1;
- longer-term financial forecasting — phase 2;

- external planning (reactive) — phase 3;
- strategic management — phase 4.

Not only did it transpire that CASE was set in the phase 1/phase 2 mode historically (save for the abandoned attempts at phase 3 several years previously), but the style of planning which seemed to be behind the top team's recent halting attempts in late 1989/early 1990 was phase 2 with some hints of phase 3. In short, it was perceived that besides the problems encountered on process there were also some doubts as to whether any robust 'strategic' plan would be ultimately arrived at.

This unease was reinforced by the early output from the top team's SWOT analysis. Not surprisingly, this SWOT analysis revealed a wealth of issues of a highly uncertain nature concerning market technology, regulatory trends and competitive activity. The planning tools which they had used to date (SWOT analysis, Gap analysis), although valuable, did not seem to be up to the task of grappling with these uncertainties.

It is a brave management team which changes horses (or consultants) in midstream, but in very late spring 1990, the team elected to use the second consultant to help them deliver a strategic plan.

Strategic planning rarely happens as is told in the textbooks and the following description reflects this fact. The start of the strategic review was delayed by two-weeks, because the business development director was on holiday (with hindsight this was just as well, given the scale of the task ahead). On day one, the consultant and business development director (still recovering from jet lag) met to formulate a 'plan-for-the-plan'.

After a one-day session with the director's room barred and bolted, a first-cut view of the process (which subsequently became Figure 7.1) was drawn up. This fast progress was possible as the SWOT analysis had been regrouped into a small number of 'Key Strategic Issues' which would then form the focus for task forces within Dowty CASE. These issues were subsequently refined throughout the review as a 'competitive SWOT analysis'. By the end of the analysis it was remarkable how much the original SWOT had been changed by competitive analysis. This highlighted that certain apparent strengths were not 'strengths' if measured in a competitive context, whilst certain weaknesses were not really weaknesses at all.

Despite many aspirins and cigars, after two further days of incarceration the two key players had grown to know one another better

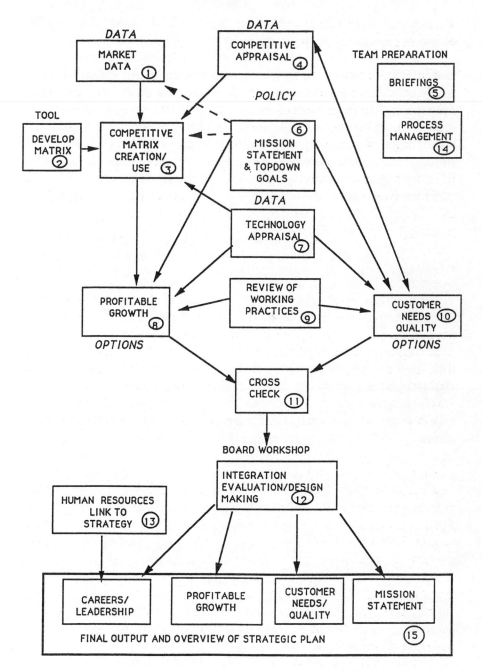

Figure 7.1 Dowty case business plan

and had crystallised a more detailed vision of the process which would deliver a strategic plan by the end of September 1990.

The process for arriving at the plan stole the imagination of the Dowty Communications top management team, raising expectations that this would generate sufficient strategic insight to drive the business forward. Two weeks later, a presentation was made to 60 managers to tell them what the process was and how they would be asked to help. During the presentation the consultant placed particular emphasis on the three essential ingredients of successful strategic planning and change: analysis, choice and implementation (Johnson, 1988). The consultant said very clearly to a packed audience:

> Although it will be difficult, you will find the analysis phase difficult but challenging and enjoyable; the choice phase much more difficult and perhaps painful; and the implementation phase the hardest of all.

With hindsight, the consultant wished that he had emphasised this message even more — managers need to understand this key fact about strategic planning not just in their heads but also in their hearts and even their stomachs. Six months later he heard it said from at least one quarter that 'We never really expected that the strategic plan would generate changes which required so much effort to implement'.

Having set the scene for the launch of a strategic review implicitly aimed at generating strategic change, let us now turn to the analysis phase.

PLANNING AND LEARNING — ANALYSIS

During the analysis phase about 80 managers and staff were involved in analysing Dowty's market attractiveness and competitive position. Managers provided input to a number of product/market analyses using a tailored version of the General Electric (GE) matrix which plotted market attractiveness against competitive position (for more details on how to use this see Grundy, 1992).

This tool proved to be extremely valuable in separating the:

1. judgements in relative market attractiveness from
2. judgements in relative competitive advantage.

During this analysis a set of ten criteria were established for 'market attractiveness' and ten for 'competitive position'. The findings from this analysis (which was captured in a computerised database in order to facilitate further sensitivity analysis and evaluation) were:

- In many areas Dowty's prior views about its competitive position were misleading.
- Despite a wealth of pre-existing quantitative market data, the process revealed, through segmented Dowty's markets geographically and by product, a substantial gap in data on certain markets which were now being penetrated as an emergent strategy (Mintzberg, 1978).
- Dowty Communications also discovered that its implicit product/market average was far more extensive and complex than had previously been realised, raising the issue of how clearer focus on 'what business we are in' could be restored and sustained without losing altogether the flexibility of an entrepreneurial management style.

This partly qualitative data was subsequently tested against:

- a high-level customer survey of their perceived positioning of the organisation against certain key competitors;
- an internal analysis of Dowty's competitive strengths and weaknesses (in what was called the 'working practices' project);
- input by a number of staff who had recently joined from competitors, which was particularly enlightening.

The planning team was thereby able to measure the organisation's competitive position in a number of dimensions using qualitative data from a number of sources.

It was also intended to use these grids to measure progress in improving Dowty's competitive advantage, and also as a means of evaluating the intangible benefits of investment decisions in an on-going fashion.

This 'analysis' phase required a large resource input, but the learning impact on the organisation was considerable, if intangible. At this stage there appeared few barriers on the surface to resisting new insights.

With hindsight, the focus for this analysis might have been narrowed down more by the top team. However, the concern was to produce a 'strategy' which would be credible — this demanded completeness. It subsequently transpired, however, that the analysis phase in itself had drained perhaps 50 per cent of the organisation's short-term energy and capacity for both undertaking and implementing the strategic review. This manifested itself at the critical 'implementation of change' phase when managers' behaviour showed visible signs of exhaustion with the process.

On the other hand, any attempt at prior scoping-down of the review by the top team might have been perceived by senior managers as pre-judging those markets which should be vigorously attacked, and which products should be pushed hardest.

This highlights the penalties of developing a complex business on an incremental basis (Quinn, 1980) without clear strategic overview: the task of organisational learning to achieve a 'catch-up' strategic vision can be considerable. This emphasises that strategic planning is best undertaken not as a 'big bang' kick-start to strategic change involving a 'leap forward', or as a 'catch up' to understand external markets, but should be a continuing feed-in to incremental development.

PLANNING AND LEARNING — CHOICE

During the hot summer of 1990, the managers of Dowty CASE worked late into the evening and at weekends to deliver plan outputs on time according to a detailed critical path. By August 1990, the analysed and semi-cooked choices (in the form of 'suggested options') were crystallis-ing ready for the top team's 'decision workshop' (again, see Figure 7.1).

This workshop was scheduled to be a two-day event, which, in the view of the consultant and the business development director, seemed too short. Both believed that three days (at least) were required to deal with the number and complexities of choice facing the organisation. Also, it was advised that the workshop should be off-site. In the event, due to logistics and other reasons, the top team met for two days in the more basic, and perhaps less inspiring, environment of a room in the company's main operations facility. This proved difficult to insulate from other day-to-day activities, and was also perhaps too visible, ratcheting expectations that 'something is about to happen' a notch further. On the positive side, time was taken out to unwind and reflect at a dinner which was held off-site.

During these two hot and intensive days, a concerted attempt was made to hammer out the major strategic choices facing the organisation.

The key successes of this process were:

- The decision was taken to put efforts for high growth behind certain activities and to sustain others at lower rates of growth.
- The organisation's 'competitive style' (differentiation, cost leadership or 'best-cost', 'industry-wide' versus 'focus') was determined in relation to each product and service grouping (Porter, 1985).
- The issue of conflict or tension between differences or shades in CASE's generic competitive strategies was explored.
- The country-by-country and product-by-product strategy focus was decided.
- Actions to restore focus to the business were agreed and also on how opportunism would be channelled to ensure that tactical moves did not undermine the entire strategy while keeping it 'partly-fluid'.

However, in two days it was unrealistic to gain 100 per cent ownership and commitment to these decisions. It was quickly realised that this would only occur through surfacing the main implications (or 'implementation issues') of these decisions in full. The top team, therefore, moved on to a series of ongoing half-day workshops beginning at 4 pm over the next week to ensure that implementation issues were evaluated (Piercy, 1989). In total, the original plan for two days turned into 53 hours of ongoing debate to surface and address the main implications of the decisions.

Major sticking points which slowed down the process of choice were:

- The choice of generic competitive strategies presumed a clear understanding of the difference between a differentiation and cost leadership (or 'best-cost' strategy). At this point, definitions from Porter's 'competitive advantage' were used explicitly, presented in a series of overheads. These highlighted that cost leadership meant being *the* lowest cost supplier, whilst differentiation meant adding sufficient value to command some price premium relative to competitors. It was pleasing to find that Porter's definitions were clear (despite attempts by other theorists to suggest that his generic choices are over-simplified), although perception of the meaning of these strategies was fuzzy (Bowman, 1992). However, it was found that, even once the learning barriers were overcome so that managers understood how the generic strategies differed, there was a tendency to prefer a 'differentiation' strategy in an area where cost leadership was more appropriate. This was more consistent with the organisation's self-image and its underlying 'paradigm'.

- Out of the large number of decisions, one concerned an important operational area — the sales force. The top team spent almost a whole day on this issue which, from the point of view of delivery of all the key outputs from the process, might have been regarded as a digression. However, the salesforce issue was at the heart of the organisation's strategic paradigm or 'how we do things around here' (see later discussion on 'implementation of change'). It was also crucial to its operational and market survival. It was, therefore, a natural area for in-depth focus, although there was clearly an opportunity cost of spending on this one issue.
- It proved particularly hard to get agreement to cessation of certain areas of business activity. Although this was tied into business control measures to ensure that it actually happened (see next section), there were signs that these messages had not got through to 'the troops' — at least in the months which immediately followed.

IMPLEMENTATION AND CONTROL OF CHANGE

At the end of the fifth mini-workshop into which the 'decision workshop' had fragmented (of what had intended to be just two days of deliberation), the consultant was asked by the managing director how he proposed the top team should now forge a process for links to action.

The consultant then said:

> It seems to me that besides adopting a strategy for renewed profitable growth, what we have uncovered here has deeper implications. We seem to have identified a number of major changes in the organisation which are essential to make this profitable growth happen, especially in the face of intensifying competitive pressure, customers who are becoming increasingly discerning and with an accelerating rate of obsolescence in products and technology. I am afraid to say again (as I warned in June 1990) that the links to implementation will be hard, especially as what we are now about is clearly a process of strategic change.

The managing director readily took to this signal and steps were set in place to ensure that the 'links to action' not only happened but were 'cemented' immediately. These included:

- A number of 'change initiatives' would be set up, focused on the issues identified through the strategic planning process where there was a need or opportunity to improve Dowty's competitive position.
- All managers would be told to revisit their budgetary submissions with a view to reflecting the requirements now emerging from the strategic plan output. (Although this produced some grumbles from middle managers, the consultant argued that it should be put to them that this enabled a 'before' and 'after' the strategic plan comparison to be done.)
- The strategic plan would be communicated to senior managers at a series of informal presentations.
- A platform for strategic change (Ansoff) would be created by the personnel director working in tandem with the consultant through a series of three-day workshops on 'Competitive Advantage and Change Management'. During these workshops, managers performed their own mini-strategic analysis of the organisation's competitive position and analysed key implementation issues which included: international strategy, technology development, investment decision-making, cost-savings, organisational culture and paradigm, etc. (This was useful in spreading ownership of the overall rationale for the strategy although it did not, in itself, gain ownership to the specifics.) Managers were provided with a small number of implementation tools such as forcefield analysis and stakeholder analysis (Piercy, 1989) which were found invaluable. In fact, so successful were these workshops that the top management team wanted to go through this process for themselves, even though they had already worked through the top team strategic workshop process. Pressures of time, along with the understandable feeling that they had 'seen just one workshop too many', prevented them from doing this.
- A framework for 'strategic controls' would be instigated which would be used to track strategic implementation on a quarterly basis. These controls were blended with operational and financial controls (to avoid duplication) as a set of 'key business measures'.
- A framework of interlocking objectives for all departments and managers would be put in place so that all micro-level behaviour would be aligned to deliver the strategic plan.

- Entrepreneurial and innovative behaviour would be channelled so that the strategic change process would not conflict with the organisational culture which was individualistic and entrepreneurial.
- The question as to whether, and if so to what extent, the strategic change process should embrace culture change was agreed to be an issue for subsequent examination.

The reader may have noted that the strategic plan itself was merely one output to the process. This plan was documented in several ways in order to focus the communication process on a number of targeted audiences:

- Overheads on the key strategic decisions and their implications and a more detailed product-by-product and country-by-country set of (about 25) strategies.
- A more lengthy document (50 pages) defining mission and goals, external environment, current competitive position, key strategic decisions and the implications for change in organisational focus, and for operational infrastructure and human resources development. Last, but not least, was a set of broad financial projections which would serve as longer-term financial measures of success along with investment requirements. This document was owned by the management team and selected parts were circulated freely to reports down the organisation, overcoming earlier 'secrecy' concerns.
- A simplified, higher level overview of the strategic plan was created of a dozen overheads for presentation to senior managers. This presentation was delayed due to internal uncertainties associated with a pending re-organisation at Divisional level. This reorganisation inevitably diminished somewhat the impact of the communication process. It also highlighted the need for timely roll-out to meet expectations previously created in the organisation that 'something is about to happen', and soon.

Looking back, the length of 'the strategic plan' caused the consultant some minor embarrassment, as this runs counter to much later thinking on 'strategic planning' and 'strategic thinking' which puts a great premium on brevity. However, given the complexity of Dowty's business, the need to spell out the implications of the strategy in detail and in order to provide clear enough links to implementation, brevity had to be partly sacrificed. Interestingly, middle managers who gained access to the 'full plan' said that it was more helpful and specific than the much shorter presentation material. All of this stresses that communication of any change, particularly of a strategic nature, needs most careful thinking through. This phase warranted a 'planning module' in its own right.

So far, the list of approaches to strategic change may sound like a textbook case, perhaps reminiscent of 'In Search of Excellence' stories, although the reader will have detected a number of imperfections from which the management team and myself have learnt. But corporate life in the early 1990s is harder than the picture painted by US management evangelists, and well-intentioned strategic change endeavours have to cope with perhaps increased, rather than reduced, turbulence. During the period between late 1990/early 1991 — when initial steps to implement the plan were being taken — the top team had to wrestle with:

- a major reorganisation within the rest of Dowty plc's IT division with major implications for CASE;
- the full bite of the post-Lawson recession;
- Dowty Group's own prospects were weakened by the full effect of a slump in the defence industry (despite the Gulf War).

During the bleak and icy period of the winter 1990/91, the heady, visionary days of the hot 1990 summer may have appeared a nirvana. Despite these icy winds of turbulence and set-backs in many areas of strategic change, Dowty Communications persisted in efforts to implement the central insights on where it wanted to go, how it might get there and how it might need to do things differently to get there. Although its original ambitions needed to be moderated somewhat in the light of external change, teams continued to work on implementing critical areas of change throughout 1991 (when the strategy was revisited and communicated to all employees) and into 1992. Particular successes were in the areas of simplification and in making the organisation more cost-competitive.

Interestingly, an area of strategic change which appeared to prove most robust during these difficult times was the area of strategic measures or controls which were integrated with operational or tactical measures within a small number of 'key business measures'. These were tangible areas where Dowty Communications was beginning to manage its business in more strategic fashion.

CONCLUSIONS

Having presented the case history, it is now opportune to try to make sense of this case in relation to an earlier model of strategic change by using the previous ideas of the three important elements in managing strategic change — strategy, structure and culture. To this framework three key interlinking elements have been added, namely:

- between strategy and culture — the MISSION;
- between culture and structure — the PARADIGM;
- between strategy and structure — LEADERSHIP.

The Dowty's strategic change process appears to be characterised as:

- triggered originally by perceived need to establish a STRATEGY as an enabling device for LEADERSHIP;
- which subsequently generated structure issues which were then fed into the reorganisation process;
- but the subsequent reorganisation of STRUCTURE disrupted the launch of the STRATEGY on its implementation platform;
- while in setting up the implementation platform issues about CULTURE were surfaced, particularly their links to STRUCTURE, ie the PARADIGM (or 'how we do things around here');
- these PARADIGM issues were felt to add too much to a burden of change and were, therefore, re-scheduled for subsequent action rather than tackled immediately;
- thus effectively putting the organisation back into a more usual mode of incremental change mode by early spring 1991.

Following the upheaval generated by the strategic review and reorganisation, management resumed their style of 'business as usual'. However, strategic change has refused to go away. Dowty Communications is continuing to manage this strategic change but perhaps at a less frenetic pace. This period of turbulence followed by a return to more continuous change is a characteristic of change in other organisations (Johnson, 1992).

The case history of Dowty Communications is thus resonant with lessons on how strategic planning can be used as a vehicle to drive strategic change, as well as how it needs to embrace structure and culture, and particularly the underlying paradigm. Key lessons include:

- Any strategic planning process must balance having a fit with the organisation against the need to stretch its vision.
- Unless a strategic planning process generates or steers strategic decision-making and internal change, it is not truly 'strategic' (thinking the problem with number-led approaches).
- Senior managers may be tempted to begin a 'strategic planning' process without full realisation of a) the full extent of what it might reveal (either externally or internally), or b) that the need for major, strategic change may emerge from this process and also of the need to link strategy, structure and culture through leadership, paradigm shift and an appropriate mission.
- Successful strategic planning involves endless attention to getting the planning process right (for example, being participative, pro-active, cross-functional, iterative, creative etc).
- Getting the process right is a necessary but insufficient condition of success: content and analysis tools are absolutely vital and should be introduced on a 'just-in-time basis' throughout to prevent learning overload.
- Whilst strategic planning can generate an enormous wealth of learning, the effect of behavioural barriers and the elapse of time can cause an equally fast process of unlearning (making strategic change akin to a kind of 'snakes and ladders').
- The communication process requires as much planning and effort as does the original plan. It should also be targeted at different segments of stakeholders — the top team, senior managers, employee groupings, corporate centre and external customers and collaborators (the same fundamental message needs to be tuned to the different receiver).
- Setting expectations about the duration and the effort required needs to be made forcibly, consistently and continuously throughout the process.
- Strategic planning and strategic change involve complex or 'double-loop' learning (at every stage) and managers should be constantly reminded of that fact and understand that this means they are out of usual managing mode, and that this can be very tiring.
- Managers must be alert to imminent storms (recessions, reorganisations) which may blow the strategic change process off course.
- Cultural change or shift is an issue which should never be 'out-of-play', and it is unwise to block these issues. Indeed, culture change

was put back onto the agenda at Dowty Communications in 1991.

- When beginning to implement strategic change, the top team should again begin to 'let go', by delegating key strategic change projects to senior managers (thus avoiding overload and to bolster commitment to change).
- Any opportunity for change must be seized quickly and effectively, otherwise it will rapidly disappear (especially one created through learning workshops for implementing strategic change).
- Strategic planning, learning and change is a one-way ticket: once embarked on you cannot go back without being worse off than if you had never started on the journey. In addition, top management's expectations about the amount of effort, degree of attention and the duration involved in managing strategic change via a strategic planning intervention need to be skilfully managed.

Before we conclude this case, it may be worthwhile to explore how some of the 'managing change' tools were used in addition to those of 'strategic analysis' to manage this process.

The relevant change tools which were used included:

- The 'five stage' model of diagnosis, planning, implementation, control and learning reflects closely the stages of data collection and analysis, strategic decision-making and programming of change. Also, 'strategic controls' combined controls with learning in one. More specifically, the change initiatives were defined to segregate the phases of 'diagnosis' and 'planning'. This was found invaluable as, in several areas, the nature of the problem had not been fully understood.
- Force field analysis was used extensively to surface enablers and barriers within each change thrust.
- Stakeholder analysis was used to identify and track key influencers on the change process including players within the 'top team'.
- Project processes were used to programme each change thrust as a clearly identified 'project'.

As a final note, the organisation used a number of 'change' agents to progress the change. Besides the earlier consulting team and the second consultant's involvement, a further consulting firm was engaged to help make progress on detailed implementation efforts during 1991. By early 1991 the change agent (the second consultant) felt it was preferable for the team to seek new input to amplify the message that 'change must now move forward'. The change agent may go down in history as being one of the few consultants who suggested his own exit when his symbolic role as a 'change catalyst' had reached saturation.

Final lessons for the reader from this case are that:

- Strategic planning can provide a powerful impetus to the change process provided that it is seen not merely as an analysis process but one involving challenge to an organisation's self-concept and behaviour.
- This can only succeed if strategic planning is managed as a change process from the outset, and if expectations about the effort required to move it forward are sensitively and continuously managed.
- Change tools can be invaluable in moving around blocks (particularly 'stakeholder analysis') and can be used to defuse tension through humour in workshops.
- Softer aspects including 'the paradigm' and culture are important, not only because they influence perceptions of strategic position but also because these play a central role in determining competitive advantage.
- The prime mover for change may itself change during the process — not only any external change catalyst, but also within the top team itself (which in this example went through two major changes).

Postscript

In 1992 Dowty Group was acquired by TI. Dowty Communications was subsequently sold to Cray and was re-named Cray Communications.

8

STRATEGIC CHANGE AT PRUDENTIAL LIFE ADMINISTRATION

INTRODUCTION

Prudential Life Administration (or 'Life Administration') is the administrative centre which services the Prudential's direct UK sales force. The Prudential has been famous for many decades for 'The Man from the Pru' who calls into UK households on a regular basis. With its direct sales force, the Prudential services a large market share of the UK life insurance market via its 'Home Service' Division. This generates a large workload of administration which is serviced from 'Life Administration' at Reading — an important part of Home Service Division.

This case focuses on a major change over the late 1980s and early 1990s to make Life Administration more responsive, effective and lower cost. This involved transforming a traditional, somewhat inward-looking organisation of some 2000 staff into a flatter, fitter and faster organisational unit. This is described as follows:

- the context for change;
- mobilising for change;
- reflecting on change — mid-course correction;
- making structure and style change work;

- review and learning;
- summary of outputs and outcomes and lessons.

THE CONTEXT FOR CHANGE

During the 1950s, 1960s and 1970s the life insurance market grew substantially, with the Prudential maintaining a strong position in this market. This was helped by its substantial direct sales force. In the 1980s a number of factors began to have an impact, which were to reshape the industry, particularly:

- an economic boom fuelled by a variety of social, monetary and political factors;
- de-regulation in the financial services industry generally;
- competition intensifying from UK banks and building societies;
- fiscal encouragement by the Conservative Government to encourage saving and wider investment in shares, personal pension schemes and other savings vehicles;
- the pending threat of 1992 and the reduction of national barriers within Europe.

By the mid to late 1980s, the external environment for Prudential Home Services appeared to become more mixed. On the one hand, there was a surge of growth in the life insurance industry generally but the sustainability of that growth, as well as the relative market shares of key players, was looking increasingly uncertain. This was particularly true in relation to personal pensions following legislation changes which made these much more attractive to customers.

It might, therefore, have been easy to continue to seek improvements within Life Administration as a service function within Home Service on an incremental basis, without considering more fundamental change. But senior management within the Prudential believed that Life Administration was of such strategic importance that a 'steady improvement' policy would be inappropriate. There was also concern that in order to compete into the 1990s it was crucial to improve the quality of service and to improve its cost effectiveness. This suggested a major intervention to make Life Administration a leaner, effective and efficient organisation.

There were more specific internal triggers for intervention. In the late 1980s the Prudential launched a number of new products and demand outstripped expectations in the heady economic climate of that time. Almost overnight, Life Administration was faced with major increases in throughput, putting strain on its processing capability. In the short run, this led to operating difficulties and temporary backlogs which underlined to senior management the need to improve responsiveness of the organisation. There was also a feeling that the error rate associated with transaction processing, although acceptable in the past, was in excess of that required to compete effectively into the 1990s, given the improvements which competitors would certainly be making.

The task of change was of major proportions. Life Administration then employed 2,000 staff in a relatively complex and hierarchical structure. The culture of Life Administration was said to be 'traditional' and 'paternalistic' which could result in considerable inertia or even active resistance in the face of a sustained change intervention. The task of shifting Life Administration into being a flexible, responsive, quality-led yet cost effective organisational unit appeared daunting.

In terms of Life Administration's paradigm, the changes envisaged were as follows:

PARADIGM	From	To
POWER	Restricted	Resides at the lowest appropriate level
STRUCTURE	Hierarchical	Flatter
CONTROLS	Instinctive and seat of pants	Measured objectives
ROUTINES	Retrospective looking	Live and forward looking
RITUALS	Loose plans	Structured plans
MYTHS	The 'Mighty Pru' 'Life Administration is OK'	Real world
STORIES	Our job well done	Delighted customers
SYMBOLS	Status hierarchy	Rewards for performance
MANAGEMENT STYLE	Aloof	Open

To summarise, the key objectives of change were to:

- turn Life Administration from being an average performing administrative centre to one excelling in service quality and yet at a low cost as the 'engine room of the Prudential';
- whilst retaining key elements of the culture which made Life Administration an 'attractive' place to work; however, the emphasis would be on 'attractiveness' in terms of 'challenge and fun' rather than 'cosy and secure';
- to effect this change while ensuring continuity of Life Administration's operations — the change would be conducted with least disruption.

MOBILISING FOR CHANGE

We now turn to the steps taken to mobilise for the change. In common with many strategic change initiatives, a key signal of pending change was the appointment of a new head of Life Administration. In his mid 30s, with a background as an economist and actuary, Tom Boardman was given the daunting task of moving Life Administration from a 'me-too' organisation to a centre of excellence, in terms of both quality and efficiency of service.

Although Tom had a more technical professional background as an actuary, he was keenly interested in management practice and people motivation. During his time as head of Life Administration from 1989 to 1991, he held regular sessions where a member of senior and middle management would present some 'ideas on best management practice' that they had distilled from a number of books or articles. These sessions were focused on specific issues in Life Administration.

Tom Boardman was an enthusiast for using best management practices to drive the change process. From February 1988 through to April 1991 he, along with the management team, initiated a number of major change thrusts which included:

- devising a 'mission' for Life Administration which would provide a focus for the change. This was developed by a group of managers who went away for nearly a week to think about quality out of which came the key ideas within 'the mission';
- learning more about perceptions of Life Administration by undertak-

ing detailed market research and continuing to track these perceptions as a 'control' for change;

- launching a major quality programme with the aim of creating a
measurable quantum shift in the quality of the organisation's outputs
and processes;

- re-focusing business plans in order to drive change through
performance measures to replace existing budgets for 'more of the
same'. Quality measures were to provide the heart of the business
plans;

- installing a project management process for managing specific areas
of change.

Besides these change thrusts, a number of new managers were brought
in at both senior and middle levels to inject new ideas and energy into the
management team. A number of these new managers were young and had
joined the Prudential in recent years.

The quality programme was, therefore, an important plank in the
change strategy. In order to provide a solid foundation for the programme, surveys of how customers saw Life Administration were
conducted. The results provided reinforcement to internal messages of
the change imperative, as well as a means of ongoing measurement.

Linked to the concept of quality was a major effort to measure the
efficiency and effectiveness of service to customers and of internal
operations. This involved strengthening the business planning unit to co-
ordinate market research, performance measures and the quality
programme. By focusing these key initiatives under one manager it was
possible to bring much greater cohesion and singularity of direction to
the change process.

So far, the scale of change which was being contemplated may seem
nothing extraordinary. However, to underline the magnitude of the
change task it is worthwhile to reflect on the sheer size of the Life
Administration machine. Some salient facts which highlight the scale of
activities are that Life Administration:

- services 15 million policies each year;
- handles 18 million items of mail annually;
- receives 100,000 telephone calls each month.

This workload was achieved through a highly complex set of systems and
administrative processes with a traditional workforce and many tiers of

management. This highlights the scale of the task of transforming the organisation (with least disruption) into a fighting force.

It is hardly surprising, therefore, that it took the best part of two years to mobilise fully for change. This was, in part, due to the decision to phase structure changes *after* the start of the quality roll-out, as it was feared that to push forward on both initiatives simultaneously would have been counterproductive. The new management team, under Tom Boardman, also probably underestimated the time and sustained effort required to mobilise for this change. Indeed, it was not until around mid to late 1990 that it became apparent that there was still a long way to go in sustaining change initiatives so as to reap the underlying benefits of the whole programme. As was put recently by Kippa Alliston, Tom Boardman's successor:

> A lot has been achieved in the last 18 months in moving Life
> Administration towards a total quality, customer-led culture
> where we're selling not just a product, but service excellence
> itself. It will take another three years or so for that culture to
> put down deep roots.

It became clear during 1990 that the really sticky areas of change were of a more behavioural rather than of a more tangible nature. Although the initiatives co-ordinated by the business planning unit were beginning to bear fruit, a number of symptoms of barriers to change began to become apparent. For instance, during the first business planning cycle managers lapsed into their old 'budget games' — putting in excess and spurious bids for resources which they knew would be negotiated away. This was despite Tom Boardman clearly laying the ground rules that budgets would be based on 'business' rather than on territorial needs. Although the quality programme was making headway, there also seemed to be some blocks within the management team itself which inhibited this initiative from being taken seriously.

Tom Boardman felt that it was now time to 'up the ante' and looked to focusing an attack on behavioural style through a 'Managing Change Programme' — which we now turn to.

REFLECTING ON CHANGE — MID-COURSE CORRECTION

In Spring 1990 a small team of management developers within the Prudential began to think about staging an organisational learning intervention in Life Administration. This was aimed at producing an 'organisational shock' which would unblock the barriers to change through a top team learning vehicle. The task of co-ordinating this intervention was given to an external consultant and an experienced management developer familiar with the problems and opportunities of linking management development and organisational change. The initiative was focused on overcoming the blocks to change and is expanded on at greater length here because it highlights the difficulties of managing blocks and barriers: this was merely a part of the overall change dynamic.

It would have been tempting to send the management team off to a famous business school for a week to learn (intellectually) about managing change. Instead, the argument was put (and accepted) that this was unlikely to be effective in generating behaviour shift as opposed to just being a learning exercise. At the same time, it was decided that the legitimacy of a 'business school' framework for managing change was secured so that managers would not simply reject messages as 'superficial and untested'. An independent consultant was then asked by Tom Boardman to help Life Administration run these change workshops.

Through previous work in learning interventions as vehicles for triggering organisational change, the consultant was acutely aware of the potential limitations of this approach. Where only some rather than all of the management team are involved, there is uneven ownership of new concepts, beliefs and behaviours. Individual learning can also rapidly fold-back on itself (the 'unlearning process') unless some active experimentation with change frameworks is undertaken.

Instead of a conventional development programme, an action-based-change programme was set up. This involved:

- extensive discussions with Tom Boardman (as key stakeholder) to focus the programme, to determine desired learning and behavioural change, to identify key strategic change issues and areas where specific action would be necessary;
- interviews with half a dozen of the management team to include both the 'new blood' and the 'old blood';
- design of a two-day workshop (run twice for a dozen managers in each workshop) on 'Managing Change'. All of the top management team attended this workshop programme. This involved working through two cases — managing strategic change at British Rail and at

BP using the change tools explored earlier in this book. These cases were used to begin the 'unfreezing process'. (The BP case was based on publicly available material in the *Financial Times* written by Christopher Lorenz.) On the second day of each workshop a set of 'change issues' were input (distilled from pre-interviews with Tom Boardman and with a 'representative sample' of the management team) to stimulate debate on 'a strategic vision for Life Administration'. These 'issues' were at the core of the workshops: prior to this these had been more implicit and less than fully shared within the management team;

- four 'learning and change projects' were devised for managers to work on as learning vehicles. These incorporated similar issues to those which had already been addressed by the business planning unit whose head, Andrew Budge, provided helpful ammunition for the learning and change workshops. (This was an excellent example of internal and external change catalysts working in close partnership.) The 'problem' within each project was then pre-identified by Tom Boardman with some external input. Each of these four projects involved group work in workshops by a team of six managers over a two-month period meeting;

- finally, a two-day 'Change Conference' was run for all the management team, over 21 managers. In these two days the output of each learning and change project was presented and debated. The conference was attended by Tom Boardman's boss, a senior director of Prudential Home Service.

During the short design phase, Tom Boardman quickly realised the potential of the programme. Although the programme was initially seen perhaps as a 'pure' learning programme, the benefits of addressing live critical business and organisational issues came quickly to the fore. Not only did this involve running an individual development and team-building programme, it also involved analysing and moving towards resolving some key change issues. As these were both pressing and (part) tangible, this, in turn, enabled blocking management behaviours to be flushed out and made visible.

In mobilising for change generally it is essential to link change initiatives and projects explicitly, rather than to assume these linkages speak for themselves. This enables the change to be time-compressed, as otherwise initiatives may meander towards their goals. During the Life

Administration change workshop it was remarkable (even to the consultant) how much the change process could be accelerated through an organisational learning 'hot-house'.

For instance, during the second two-day workshop a new learning (and change) project emerged during the analysis. One syndicate group had been given the task of analysing the issues associated with changing the roles of the first-line supervisor. From the top team's perspective, this area of change had been recognised but had not been (at that point) seen as having both a high impact and being extremely difficult to implement. The syndicate performed a force field analysis and reported back with a diagram which was more adverse than the one which they had done for a 'very difficult change' (a previous syndicate exercise exploring change at British Rail).

Several of the managers were physically shaken as they came out of their syndicate room — clearly a key insight (however negative) had emerged. The rest of the management team were able (through using the force field analysis tool) to share the syndicate's vision of the change and to confirm that this appeared both vitally important and also uncertain. The force field also highlighted the process levers which would help the change move forward. These included defining the change objective more tightly and deriving a strategy for change which built ownership rather than alienated key stakeholders.

By 9.30 am on the Monday following the second change workshop (Thursday and Friday of the previous week), Tom Boardman had set up a new change project based on this syndicate's output — the 'Structure Project'. This was to be managed by an experienced change manager seconded from his line role on a full-time basis. At the time of writing (spring, 1992) this manager is still full-time project manager whose principal responsibility is to implement the 'Structure Project'.

Other key insights also emerged which were promptly set in action. For instance, although Life Administration had set up a project management process by late 1990 the linkages and interdependencies between change projects were implicit rather than explicit. A second key task of the Manager, Structure Project, was to map these interdependencies, to identify any overlaps and to (where necessary) re-configure projects. Surprisingly, this took several weeks to accomplish, highlighting how important it is to identify interdependencies between change projects from the outset.

Moving on to the 'Change Conference' which involved all top 21 managers, in the past, Life Administration had held an annual conference which was, typically, an inward-looking event, focusing on operational issues. It had been planned to run a one and a half day 'feedback workshop' to end the Change Programme. Tom Boardman saw the opportunity, however of achieving two objectives with one vehicle and announced that the annual conference would become a 'Change Conference'. The two-day event would be facilitated externally.

Managers are often attracted to content-led issues and it was determined, therefore, that to balance this we would have equal emphasis on process during the conference. This would include the project team's reflections on their own learning process (including openness to change). A critique was thus made not only on the content of their projects but also on how they worked together as teams — in other words, their process. This enabled the top management team to gain an insight overall into their openness as an organisational unit to learning and challenge. By playing back external 'impressions' it was possible for the facilitator to act as a neutral organisational mirror — and without being unduly provocative. (It may be tempting for a facilitator to exaggerate weaknesses but this is a dangerous process — the facilitator quickly becomes 'the target' for externalising the team's feelings. It also produces a distortion in 'what the team sees' — just like the 'crazy mirrors' one sees at amusement arcades or fairs — exaggeration of this kind is seldom appreciated.)

The four learning and change projects which were run are illustrated in Figure 8.1. These included a project focusing on customer care, one on productivity, one on rewards and recognition and one on IT strategy. Three out of four of the projects were relatively uncontentious in content terms, save one. It is interesting to examine this closer in order to understand the underlying process at work.

One of the learning projects dealing with information technology was focused on a current change thrust which had been launched some time ago. This was of major impact on Life Administration and there was a significant degree of commitment to a particular path of action. The syndicate group highlighted that, on the face of it, there were some significant short- and medium-term problems in achieving change milestones. These milestones were critical for improving operational performance.

When the project teams presented their findings a vigorous debate began about whether these problems did or did not exist. This surfacing

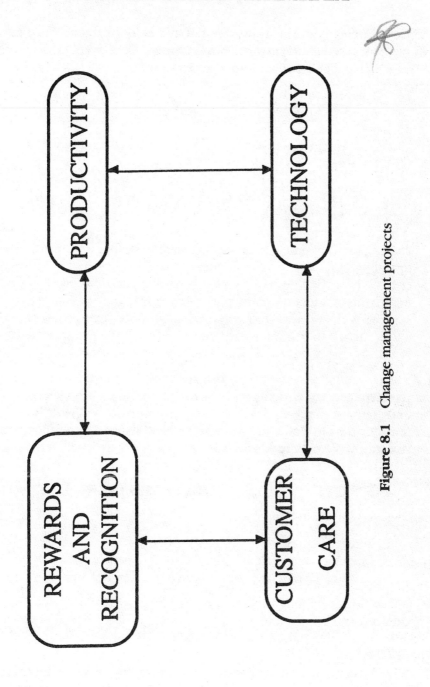

Figure 8.1   Change management projects

of contentious issues was very healthy, but the project team members felt that problems were being underplayed by members of top management.

This episode highlights a number of key lessons:

- Top management may well find it uncomfortable at times to have core business problems of a sensitive nature probed through organisational learning workshops.
- Middle managers may assume that it is top management's job to have 'all change problems' well covered — and all of the time. Yet, the complexity and ambiguity of change (especially when this involves wholesale change throughout the organisation) make this an impossible task.
- When a major issue emerges it is easy for managers to revert to 'looking for someone to blame' rather than being 'open'. The ultimate test of 'openness' involves openness to attack and when a vigorous critique is bearing down on you, it is hard to remain receptive.
- Before this incident the learning and change programme had actually run too well and too smoothly — unless some really contentious issues surface to test managers' behaviour then the programme has not really dug down to the sharp realities of managing change.

The true test of capability to manage change is not whether a management team acts defensively or openly during a workshop — it depends upon whether it subsequently goes on to re-shape how it implements change. Following the early 1991 Change Conference, the above issues were rapidly addressed.

MAKING STRUCTURE AND STYLE CHANGE WORK

Following the Change Conference, it was necessary to face the considerable difficulties of implementing change, both in organisational structure and in supporting management style. Some of these changes may have been prompted, in part, by the Change Conference and learning programme and some by ongoing thinking by the top team — change strategies are often the result of an intermingling of ideas.

Dealing first with structure, some major changes were contemplated including:

- The Life Administration structure was to be re-focused to be more outward-facing. At senior management level, one manager was responsible for interfacing with outside locations and one on internal services. Both managers were on the original management team.

- The number of senior and middle managers was reduced considerably from about 25 to 12. This involved some redeployment to other parts of the Prudential (which was pre-planned). But this still left existing managers competing for a smaller number of jobs.
- At the first-line manager level there were some major changes too, as about 100 people (from existing roles) competed for 70 jobs within the new structure. This change was conducted in parallel with a rigorous recruitment and selection process including psychometric testing and counselling of all candidates. The new roles were genuinely of a 'managerial' nature (as opposed to supervisors/technocrats).
- At the clerical level, staff were to become multi-skilled so that they would be able to do work without having frequent recourse to their supervisors to check what they were doing. As Kippa Alliston describes it: 'If ten people are all delivering one small part of the total product and it goes wrong, nobody feels accountable. If one person is accountable for all of it, you get quality and service excellence.'

A number of the above points can be amplified as follows:

First, the choice of who would become members of the new senior team was decided by a meritocratic approach. Previous incumbents were invited to apply for the new jobs. Although these changes involved considerable pain, they were accomplished with some sense of perceived fairness which did much to ease the transition.

Second, the rationale for the changes was communicated vigorously throughout the middle and lower levels of the organisation. This rationale lay in a) the rate of change in the external market; b) the need to focus on the customer; and c) the harsh financial realities which needed to be faced up to. Life Administration brought in a senior lecturer from Manchester Business School, Dr John Westwood, to give a presentation on changes in the financial services industry generally. These sessions were attended by all the administrative staff over many half-day sessions. Even so, it proved necessary to rent Reading Town Hall to accommodate the numbers of staff at each session. This emphasises the importance of spending time and effort (often lavishly) in the communication of the rationale for change.

John Westwood reflects on his sessions at Reading:

Let's not beat about the bush — before the days of Kippa Alliston and his predecessor Tom Boardman, if you put a foot out of line at Reading, you got stamped on.

If you said 'I don't know why I'm doing this — isn't there a better way?', you got squashed. All the ideas, the enthusiasm, the energy were suppressed.

Kippa's going to release them. I talked to people after the sessions and I found they were already coming up with good ideas. If you can mobilise 80 per cent of 1,800 people, you're going to get a hell of a lot of good ideas for turning Life Administration into the best and cheapest engine room in the industry.

Third, the approach taken to achieving change at the clerical worker level was one of trial and learning. Rather than impose a rigid framework of change, a degree of diversity was allowed so that the 'multi-skilling' could be tailored to different job areas. One issue which emerged was how this diversity could be managed and monitored so that Life Administration's way of doing things (its paradigm) did not become too diverse and fragmented.

The multi-skilling approach demanded a major investment in training. This ran against the earlier tradition in Life Administration that 'You don't get to do a senior job here unless you have proved yourself for years.' By intensive training, however, it proved possible to short-cut this artificially long path up the hierarchy. Training, therefore, emerged as a key vehicle in turning Life Administration into a flatter structure.

Much of this discussion has centred around structure rather than 'style'. The philosophy adopted within Life Administration was that structure and style issues were inextricable, and that changes in structure were necessarily bound together with major shifts in management style. But style was found to lag behind structure change. This was highlighted, for example, in the Change Conference in early 1991, where 'paradigm analysis' suggested that, in terms of style, the organisation was only perhaps one quarter of the way towards achieving its desired shift. A further review of progress to internalise a 'quality culture' in late 1991 also identified some remaining gaps in attitude and behaviour, although there was some dispute as to whether this was unduly pessimistic.

Given the scale of the change task already described, this pace of progress does not seem surprising. But where progress in tangible areas of change (especially in systems, structures and processes) can be achieved relatively rapidly, management becomes disappointed when soft areas of change lag behind. This may raise doubts about whether more could have been done earlier in attempting to shift style, and whether the critical path for change had been fully thought through. But had Life Administration chosen to focus on less tangible areas of change first and deferred change in more tangible areas, many of the 'hard' drivers of change would not have been engaged. This highlights the difficulty in trade-off change priorities and, equally, the sensitivity of progress to choice of where to focus, when and in what order. Kippa Alliston looks back on this change:

> Take a culture where people weren't allowed, or didn't feel empowered, to contribute — one that rewarded long service rather than ability — one that did not have a clear focus on the customer — one whose processes were designed to satisfy internal requirements . . . and then you have all the attributes of the old Prudential.

> Not enough attention was paid to the customer, whether the policyholders or those very significant other customers — the agents in the field, who in the old culture were thought of as interruptions, intrusions, people who got in the way of work, rather than as people we serve.

REVIEW AND LEARNING

By early 1992 the key planks of change were firmly in place. The management team had been slimmed down, the roles of first-line managers had been refocused and considerable progress made towards expanding the role of clerical workers. The quality programme was well bedded in and Industrial Branch, a key part of Prudential Life Administration, achieved BS 5750 recognition and won a national award for quality. Life Administration continued to perform regular market surveys to test whether perception of its customers and its responsiveness had changed.

In April 1991, Tom Boardman moved to another major change project within the Prudential. His successor appointed in May 1991, Kippa

Alliston, who had joined the Prudential from IBM, has determined to press hard with the change programme.

Tom Boardman's main achievements were to create a change culture in Life Administration from one which was resistant to change. He succeeded in thawing out much of the old organisational paradigm. His management style, which was supportive and based on team building, had an extremely good fit with this phase of change. Tom's particular contribution was to get management and staff to reflect on and own the need for change.

Kippa Alliston's style is in marked contrast — this is one of leading from the front. It is based on intense challenging which is not frightened of causing pain (both to others and to himself) — seeing this as the necessary price of moving forward quickly.

Already, mainly through natural wastage, the number of staff in Life Administration was reduced from 2,000 in 1989 to about 1,600 by the end of 1992, while continuing to serve similar levels of workload. The rates of error in clerical work and turnaround times were also halved over the same period, even though there was a major decrease in checking.

If Tom Boardman was prepared to address change in a proactive way in Life Administration, Kippa Alliston was equally direct and explicit in taking the same programmes forward. This involved a further phase of review of progress towards meeting change objectives. This involved two major thrusts.

First, there was a review of the quality programme to establish the remaining gaps. As Kippa Alliston put it:

> We need to find out what our customers want and how they want to be served — and one thing I can predict is that whatever the customer wants, we will provide it. I want to build on the basis of customer satisfaction surveys and service-level agreements and to continue to focus all our efforts on the customer.

Second, at the time of writing all employees are undergoing a two-day customer service workshop followed up by a detailed attitude survey by external consultants. The majority of the workshops have been attended by Life Administration's head, Kippa Alliston.

Third, managers bench-marked how Life Administration was tackling the problems of making it an outward-facing, responsive and low-cost administrative service centre. Kippa Alliston puts his vision thus:

> Change into what? I describe Reading as the engine room of
> the division. That engine room, relative to its competitors,
> must become the lowest-cost engine room in the UK. And the
> highest quality.

And again:

> I am determined that Reading will become the service
> excellence centre for administration, both in terms of price
> and quality — I want success and I'm not prepared to have
> failure.

After each workshop, staff hold debriefing sessions with their managers.

The two-day customer service workshop has been well received —
principally because there have been 'no holds barred' — all staff have
been encouraged to 'tell it how it is'. This input, and particularly the
follow-up survey by external consultants, was able to highlight and
amplify a number of major tensions which were at work beneath the
organisational surface produced by the rapid pace of change. Some highly
contentious issues, such as leadership style, genuine commitment to
openness, a perceived bias towards productivity rather than service
quality emerged. The content of these findings has been fed-back to staff
in a four-page news sheet whose frankness might stun managers in more
cosy environments. The game plan (as at summer, 1992) is to distil and
connect these issues into the dozen or so key projects which will refocus
change over the next 2-3 years. In the process, it will be essential to
involve some of the more vociferous voices in turning their frustrations
into positive change.

The third task of establishing Life Administration's current position to
achieve that goal was done by establishing contacts with a number of
other leading organisations with similar administrative functions undergoing parallel change. In this bench-marking exercise, the new
management team began by posing a dozen key questions which focused
on both the content and process of managing change in a complex
administrative centre. These questions were also used in the 'look-alike'
organisations prior to establishing first-hand contact. The posing of these
questions, in itself, served as a powerful method of reflecting the progress
of changes to date. Examples of some of these questions included:

- How do we manage our (internal or external) customer from a
  distance and remain responsive?

- How do we learn from the process of change when a diversity of approaches appears to develop?
- What changes in culture are implied by this series of changes and how are these managed?
- How is the change in activities linked to system development (present and future)?
- Looking back on the change to date, how could we have done things better?

A number of important lessons can be gained from setting up this exercise:

- First, companies are eager to share experiences and approaches with non-directly competing companies. This applies not merely to implementing strategic change but to a variety of other important management issues.
- Second, companies are reluctant to seize this opportunity because of the psychological hurdle of making first contact and also of handling the experience in a structured way. By using an external facilitator it is possible to both identify target companies and contacts to network with cross-organisationally and also to establish contact.
- Third, much of the balance of the exercise lies in the critical internal bench-marking which is of great benefit in its own right.
- Fourth, when visiting other companies, managers should look for subtle differences in management processes and style which may be critical and not just hope to come away with relative performance measures such as 'better than', 'same as' or 'worse than'.

Over a three-month period, six of Life Administration's senior managers visited four major organisations in pairs, along with an external facilitator who set up contacts and structured visits. The four companies included a building society, a bank, a telecommunications group and an oil company. The issues and lessons in managing change were remarkably similar, not only within financial services, but also within the other industries networked into.

Some early insights from this bench-marking exercise were that Prudential Life Administration needed to seize the opportunity in moving to a new building (in 1993) as a way of consolidating culture change. Also, some method of harmonising change in a number of process areas, which had hitherto been empowered to seek their own solutions, needed to be applied. A renewed and more thorough-going attack on business process redesign and simplification was also necessary. There were also insights gained in how to channel the results of the employee survey into positive change and a host of indirect spin-offs on operational issues.

To conclude this case of Prudential Life Administration, the most important lesson is that a clear rationale and strategy for change must be established. This may need considerable time, effort and skill to mobilise. Besides having adequate 'change hardware' in terms of resources, project management processes, change and quality programmes, it is equally important to have 'change software'. This includes firm leadership which is prepared to be open to continuous learning; it also includes well-focused communication effort. There also needs to be some higher element to alleviate the feeling that change is burdensome. Where the organisation is shedding some of its old, bureaucratic skin in favour of greater autonomy, challenge and fun, these benefits must be continually sold to all staff.

Another central lesson is that key planks of the 'change message' such as the 'mission' need to be as simple as possible. Although the stated mission: 'Delighting our customers by delivering a quality service, in a cost-effective manner, through the contribution of everyone' may seem to be simple and clear to senior managers intellectually, it is not so easy to transmit this to all levels without some loss of impact.

Another important lesson was that managers felt they had 'communication well covered' — for example, through regular business plan updates. But what was perhaps missing, with hindsight, was 'what are the implications for me' — in other words, from the recipient's perspective?

The change journey for Life Administration is far from over. As Kippa Alliston describes it:

> It really becomes an increasingly uphill battle from now on. We have bitten the bullet on productivity and this means there really isn't the slack which we once took for granted. People are being asked to work a lot harder and for some of the staff this has proved overwhelming. In the more distant past we allowed people to drift through the levels but that is gone for ever.

> Unfortunately a lot of people joined for the old values of

security and stability and to them change has come as a painful experience. But you just can't duck that pain.

What will really help is when we get for ourselves a lot slicker set of processes. That involves stopping doing some things — for example, one of our staff had been producing a report for many, many years. Recently she said why are we doing it? It turned out that the report didn't really add a lot of value. There are those stories. But in the end we will need these systems — you can't just go around beating people up for productivity. The real challenge is to rekindle enthusiasm and build on those areas where people are doing outstanding jobs and where they really hold onto targets, rather than look at them.

The contributions of both Tom Boardman and Kippa Alliston to achieving change in Prudential Life Administration can be summed up as:

While Tom got people to think the unthinkable and got the ball rolling, Kippa Alliston picked up the ball and kicked it.

Despite some difficulties which are currently unresolved, the fact that Life Administration is moving into the later stages of this major transition without serious disruption in continuity of services or in performance bears testimony to the persistence and stamina of the (evolving) management team. No doubt, the use of change power tools combined with a quality initiative, performance measures and enlightened human resources practices played an important role, but this role would not have been effective without the refreshingly proactive style of top management.

KEY LESSONS FROM THE CASE

A number of key lessons can be distilled from the case of strategic change at Prudential Life Administration:

- Deregulation may generate rapid growth which may focus management's attention on responding to growth rather than on improving responsiveness and cost competitiveness.
- But deregulation often brings increased competitive pressure. This, in turn, provides renewed stimulus for internal improvement.

- Mobilising for change may take a considerable period to achieve, especially where culture is traditional and operations are complex.
- If strategic change is managed piecemeal and incrementally in this context it is likely to falter.
- Effective management of this kind of change requires parallel attention to *both* structure and culture alongside change in operational processes.
- A number of reinforcing interventions in the organisation are needed to shift the paradigm. These need to be 'for real' and lived-out by senior management rather than merely talked about.
- Differing leadership styles are called for by different phases of strategic change.
- Quality and customer care may provide the core of these changes, but need to be supplemented by changes in business planning, performance measurement and appraisal, external bench-marking, project management and workshops to share issues and mobilise for change.
- This shift in paradigm requires continual and genuinely 'open' internal review.
- The impact of internal review is much bolstered by external bench-marking if suitably focused and followed through.
- All of this efforts needs to be brought together within a clear and complete strategic vision embodied in firm but supportive leadership.

9

QUALITY, CULTURE AND COMPETITIVENESS AT ICL

INTRODUCTION

ICL was chosen for the third case as it illustrates and brings together most of the themes of this book. It is also an example of implementing strategic change which is now a long way down the track.

ICL is of particular interest because change was begun initially as a strategic review, followed by attempts at deliberate culture change through marketing awareness and quality management. ICL also faces difficult competitive and financial pressures, particularly in adding value to customers at least cost. Some of these pressures make it easier to implement change (through underlining the need for change); others make the change process more difficult.

The case begins by giving more background on the history of strategic change at ICL, before focusing on how quality management has been used as a change vehicle. The problem of sustaining competitiveness is then illustrated through a short, mini-case on ICL Logistics. The lessons and conclusions from the case are then distilled and evaluated.

BACKGROUND

In the early 1980s, ICL was at a watershed. The computer industry was then dominated by IBM and was principally concerned with mainframe and mini applications and the personal computer market (PC) was in its infancy. ICL had a foothold in the personal computer market, but players such as Apple and Apricot were making big gains at that end of the market.

Relative to the market leader, ICL was small and its product portfolio was not strong, nor was its hold on its key market segments in the early 1980s secure.

Rob Wilmot was brought in from Texas Instruments to inject fresh vision into ICL and in 1982 a major review of strategy was initiated. The focus of this review was on ICL's product/market strategy and also on ICL's management style.

Rob Wilmot identified that a major change in ICL's mind-set was essential in order to secure ICL's survival and success. In 1984 he commissioned a major initiative to invest in marketing skills so that all staff at ICL thought 'outside-in'. This initiative was targeted not merely at developing marketing awareness and skills but also at shifting internal attitudes. It, therefore, sought to achieve a major shift in ICL's culture.

In 1986 this change was reinforced by the launch of a company-wide quality programme. This change programme was championed by Peter Bonfield who then became chairman and chief executive of ICL. This emphasised that, in order to compete, ICL needed to forge ahead of the other small European players in delivering world-class quality.

ICL's quality programme has become (by the early 1990s) self-sustaining: a feat captured as 'The ICL way of life'. According to Trevor Mills, group quality manager, 'Unless we had really grasped the quality issue to drive change, I doubt if we would have been here today with nearly US$4 billion revenues and being the only IT company of size in Europe which is still profitable in the recession.'

Over the past couple of years ICL has made a number of significant acquisitions. It has also adapted smoothly to the transition of being owned by STC (a UK company), to having as its major parent Fujitsu, a major, world-class Japanese electronics and computing company.

As at 1992, it is planned to float ICL on the London Stock Exchange to emphasise the independence of the company. ICL will continue its links with Fujitsu, with Northern Telecom (which also owns a minority stake) and with its many other partners worldwide.

ICL's sales growth has moderated during the recent recession but has held up well relative to its rivals. Although its financial performance has been constrained by the recession, ICL claims to be the only major European IT company currently in profit.

QUALITY AND CULTURE CHANGE

Prior to 1986, quality at ICL was mainly associated with internal measurement and conformity with mainly technical requirements. The revolution in thinking which the quality programme brought about was to induce a number of shifts:

- from internal to both internal and external-facing requirements;
- from concern with a small part of value-creating activities to the total set of business processes;
- from measurement of error and corrective action to prevention of error and a philosophy of zero defects;
- from being the concern of a sub-set of operational managers to being an entire 'way of life' for managers and staff throughout the company — from top to bottom;
- from being seen as a discrete initiative to being viewed as an everlasting process of continuous improvement.

This section on quality and culture change focuses on how the programme was mobilised, the outputs of the new way of life (to date), the further challenges which are still to be overcome and the lessons for other companies.

Mobilisation for culture change

During the company-wide programme aimed at making ICL a market-led culture it was realised rapidly that the business processes and people style needed to be made much more externally responsive. Like other companies facing similar competitive challenges (for example, Rank Xerox), ICL's top management knew that unless the business could offer genuinely differentiated value to its customers its survival and success was threatened. As Trevor Mills of ICL's group quality unit put it:

> We realised that one of the major drivers of profitability was that of offering differential quality to our customers. The PIMS studies (Profit Impact of Marketing Strategy) highlighted just how important quality is as a driver of financial performance

quality. There was therefore an immediate link back into our business strategy — quality was therefore not put forward as something nice to be, but something which we must do.

In 1986 Joe Goasdoue was appointed as director of quality and corporate affairs. Joe had previously worked with British Airways to spearhead BA's quality/customer care programmes of the early 1980s. Joe advised ICL to adopt a Crosby-style philosophy of quality management, key ingredients of which were:

- Quality management needs to be implemented in totality, as total quality management (a 'TQM') to be successful.
- The idea of quality must be kept clear and simple in the concept of 'conforming to customer requirements'.
- The revolution in quality management must be perpetually sustained: this involved many of the returns being realised only 3-5 years into the programme of (persistent) change.

At first, much of the emphasis was on improving inwardly-focused performance. This was partly so as to provide a learning foundation for the rest of the initiative and partly to establish some quicker wins. However, it quickly became apparent that this scope needed to be broadened and shifted towards being much more externally orientated. There was a major shift of focus towards being more customer centred in defining and evaluating 'conformity to requirements'. This was accompanied by bench-marking key business processes against competitors ('competitive bench-marking') and against leaders in other industries ('bench-marking against best-in-class').

One of the central levers for change was ICL's recognition systems. ICL has a comprehensive system of awards for excellence for which all staff can be nominated. They can be nominated by anyone for their efforts (beyond the course of normal duty) in exceeding requirements and expectations and in genuinely 'delighting the customer'.

The system is structured in levels according to merit and achievement — gold, silver and bronze. Initially there was some scepticism that methods such as this (and the quality programme generally) would clash with the more traditional culture of the UK. However, the results of the programme have exceeded these cautious expectations. Quality at ICL has proved itself to be a natural ingredient to a culture which any visitor to ICL's sites can pick up rapidly in the buzz which pervades its people.

Turning now to the outputs from the quality process, the hallmark of the programme is that it is Results-Driven. Unlike some quality initiatives elsewhere, ICL has clearly targeted its efforts. This is encapsulated in the programme's acronym of 'SMART':

- S for Specific;
- M for Measurable;
- A for Achievable;
- R for Relevant;
- T for Trackable.

The key quality goals and milestones are communicated to carefully targeted audiences. These 'audiences' can be of considerable size and ICL prides itself on achieving full communication at low cost: it is believed that it detracts from the message when the medium is patently over-expensive or too glossy.

Results are targeted by measuring the gap between where we are now and where we want to be on a particular measurement of quality. This 'gap' is called the 'Delta' — to signify (as in mathematics) the existence of measurable increments available for continuous performance improvement.

ICL has won a number of major awards for quality in the UK and elsewhere and was the first company to be awarded British Standard 5750 company-wide in the UK. But awards are not seen as the primary goal of quality programmes or of quality professionals — they are seen as important tests of progress. They, thus, provide a source of bench-marking of achievements in the quality process.

One example of a particularly interesting application of quality management is in people development. ICL has coined the expression 'KSA' to signify that training is about improving:

- Knowledge;
- Skills;
- Attitudes.

ICL trainers and developers seek to apply 'just-in-time' thinking to training. As needs arise, training programmes are run to serve staff in a responsive manner, or, in ICL terms, as 'Just in Time Training' or JITT. There are obvious lessons which other companies can extract from this, as much training and development is delivered either on a 'just-in-case' basis or worse still, on a 'just-too-late' basis and as a remedial measure.

ICL also emphasises training in attitudes . This involves dealing with management style with key themes being those of openness, encouragement, coaching and team-working. This links in as an integral part of quality management, as staff are exhorted not to accept poor quality but to take ownership of problems to secure solutions (a tangible kind of 'empowerment').

A second area where ICL has made major improvements is in processes. This has required investment in IT and telecommunications to increase responsiveness and to reduce the costs of errors or defects. A major initiative was to improve the call-to-fix cycle. The call-to-fix cycle occurs when a system or piece of equipment experiences a defect, and there is a lag between the customer notifying ICL of this and ICL fixing it. Major strides in reducing this cycle have been achieved, partly through applying technology (for instance, by installing remote diagnosis equipment and also by faster people responsiveness). Another recent initiative following on from this success is a further initiative to reduce unscheduled maintenance. These quality projects are called 'CATs' or 'corrective action teams'.

The benefits of quality management have been felt in a number of tangible and less tangible ways:

- ICL has reduced costs where these were previously increased by the costs of poorer quality.
- Its customers have experienced a marked improvement in the quality of service — this is felt in reduced disruption to operations and less tangible cost savings in that area.
- The warm and close relationship which ICL has developed with its customer base gives it an edge in competing for new work and in protecting its existing stream of business.

These 'benefits' might be regarded with scepticism by those cautious of the hype associated with quality. As further support to the analysis, consider the following informal account by a major customer of ICL in the retail sector. This account was not made available via any ICL channel — this was a result of a chance encounter with a big player in a London change seminar:

> Oh yes, I deal a lot with ICL. They have helped us to transform
> the quality of our systems immeasurably. But we expect to be
> able to buy a good product at a sensible price from a

competent supplier . . . What I do find particularly impressive is that they really do deliver what they preach. If there is a problem, they sort it — for instance, I have had their consultants around here for several weeks before a new system goes live. And no-one started the taxi-meter clock to bill us.

Contrast this situation with what some of their rivals deliver. We also deal with one of ICL's competitors who sent us a bill for interest on an invoice which we hadn't paid within their terms. The fact that we had sent a cheque off and they had mucked it up in their system didn't seem to matter. Even though they admitted it was their error (eventually) they were insistent that we should still pay up. Talk about customer care! It obviously doesn't always reach the parts that it needs to reach in organisations.

I was so happy with ICL's flexibility that I have been sending positive messages out to the rest of Group about what they have done. Oh yes, I almost forgot, we get visits from their director of quality (Joe Goasdoue) — I believe he gets around to meet a 100 customers every year. They must really go through company cars fast there!

Another measure of what ICL has achieved in the past eight years is that there is a stream of visitors from Fujitsu, one of ICL's parents, to share learning experiences in quality management. Trevor Mills tells us:

There have been learning lessons both ways: we have learnt from them about engineering in the factory and they have learnt from us about many other business processes . . . We actually sell computer systems to them and they are a very demanding customer which is always very good for you.

Finally, ICL bench-marks quality against its rivals and also against best-in-class in adjacent industries or world-class companies in other industries.

ICL's bench-marking has proved to be an important means of gaining 'outside-in' focus to the change process. 'Bench-marking' means simply measuring the characteristics or performance of a key business process against that elsewhere. This can be done *vis-à-vis* another part of the company or (better still) by another company entirely.

ICL has a well bedded in progress for bench-marking, as per the following steps:

- Step 1 — What are we going to bench-mark?
- Step 2 — Who are we going to bench-mark against?
- Step 3 — How will we get the information?
- Step 4 — How will we analyse the information?
- Step 5 — How will we use the information?

(An example of bench-marking in ICL is given in the next section, after we have dealt with the lessons arising from quality and culture change.)

Quality and culture change at ICL

The quality programme has been used as a core vehicle for achieving culture change of a deliberate and spontaneous nature. Quality itself is not, therefore, equated with culture change, but provides an important driving force for shifting the culture. Figure 9.1 illustrates this overlap and reinforcing effect between quality management and culture change. The more direct the reinforcement there is between quality management and culture change, the more likely it is that quality will be integrated effectively in the organisation's paradigm.

To explore this further, let us go back to the 'enlarged' model of culture in the form of the paradigm from the early part of this book.

The following interrelationships illustrate the fit between the paradigm and quality management:

Examples of the paradigm	Fit with quality management
Power	Bringing empowerment
Structures	Team working
Controls	Focus on measurement
Routines	Bench-marking activities
Stories	Cases of delighting the customer
Symbols	Quality awards

The above highlights how profound an impact on the paradigm quality management can have. This is at once a threat and an opportunity — a

188

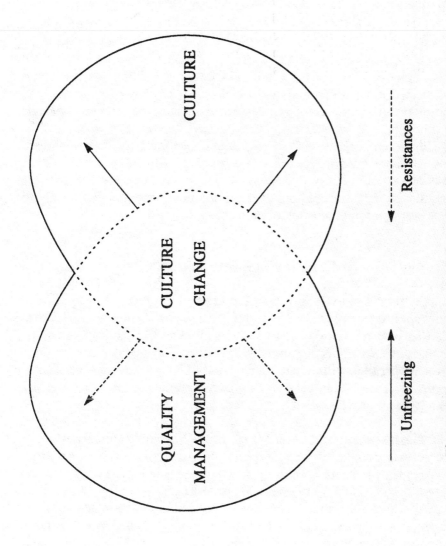

Figure 9.1 Quality management and culture change

threat because of the resistances to change which quality initiatives face for those who do not realise that these involve paradigm shift, and an opportunity through using quality as a vehicle for driving change in the paradigm.

While there have been major successes in creating a living quality culture in ICL, there remain functions — especially those responsible for marketing and sales — where more work needs to be done. As in the other cases in this book, it is often more difficult to shift the culture (and this paradigm) of those staff who are closest to the customer. These staff are often under the greatest pressure to produce quantitative results without appropriate checks — quantity may often act to drive out quality. At ICL these checks are in place — at annual appraisals, staff are judged not merely on quantitative results but also on quality of output and style.

To conclude, quality management at ICL has been used to provide impetus to shift the paradigm in a coherent manner and thereby to generate a sustained change in culture.

SUSTAINING COMPETITIVENESS

In case the ICL story sounds 'too good to be true' let us now focus on a more specific example of how strategic change has been implemented at ICL. This is an example of results-driven change aimed at sustaining competitiveness. This highlights that quality management can be practised in parallel with challenging and difficult initiatives to sustain competitiveness. This section contains a mini-case on ICL Logistics which distributes all of ICL's products in the UK.

The change began with the general manager of ICL Logistics, David Palk, and his management team at Stevenage becoming concerned about the relative competitiveness of logistics operations. In the 1980s, ICL's product mix became increasingly orientated towards smaller systems based on PCs and networks alongside larger systems, rather than primarily large mainframe and midi applications. Although the latter, larger-scale business held up, ICL logistics found itself shipping a much higher proportion of smaller products than previously. This shift occurred at the same time that competitive pressure in the PC market was intensified. Like all other functions in ICL, pressure to reduce costs mounted but ICL management were determined not to jeopardise quality and customer value.

Although David Palk and his senior management team had some ideas of what would be necessary to reduce costs — and what was achievable — he was concerned that his staff would see this as being internally imposed and arbitrary cost-cutting. He was also concerned that a top-down plan would not incorporate the ideas of his staff for effective implementation of change.

In order to gain inputs to the diagnosis phase of change, he organised a one-day workshop for 25 of his most senior staff. He began with a summary of 'where we are now' describing the performance issues faced in the logistics budget and the need for continuous improvement. He then invited a facilitator to explore how change was being managed in other companies and to provide lessons in how costs could be managed more strategically in these environments.

The workshop was then broken down into a number of multi-disciplinary teams which were invited to work on a bid for ICL's logistics business. Each team was asked to state the annual revenue at which they would be prepared to work as an independent business to service ICL's needs.

The teams worked energetically throughout the day to come up with a sensible bid which met the specification. While some members were eager to design business processes from scratch, others tended to re-invent old routines and systems, thus inadvertently giving rebirth to the old paradigm. This was held in check by others in the groups who had bought into the task more quickly.

Although the teams were facilitated to a degree, the members who were bent on radically re-shaping processes won out. Each team was then asked to present its bid. These turned out to be considerably less than the current annual costs of ICL Logistics. David Palk then revealed the figures which the management team had arrived at independently. These figures were uncannily close to those of several of the teams. Some time was spent double checking assumptions, at the end of which there was spontaneous consensus that significant cost reductions were both possible and necessary.

A further output of the workshop was a decision to bench-mark cost competitiveness so that ICL could be clearer about the available gap (or delta) for improvement, and also to learn how and what improvements could be implemented. ICL was subsequently able to test its cost levels against going rates generally in the market place and also against internal bench-marks. Fortuitously, soon after the workshop ICL acquired an IT company with low-cost distribution facilities. The ready availability of data on these costs to Logistics management ratcheted upwards by several notches the perceived need for change and improvement.

In the six months since the initial workshop, ICL Logistics has significantly reduced its workforce and is a long way to bridging its 'delta'. Its goal is to be able to serve non-ICL customers. This will show that ICL not only provides an excellent logistics service, but also achieves this at a very competitive cost.

This change has not been pain free. The story is told by David Palk:

> We spent a long, long time planning the change process and communicating the rationale — particularly in view of the loss of staff numbers. I was actually surprised that we didn't have much more resistance — it certainly pays to give even more attention to how these things are done, as opposed to what must be done. If you do cut corners then you are bound to pay later on in morale terms.

> The main surprise was that after everything had gone so smoothly, one Monday one of the guys — he was quite young — came back from his holidays. We went through the same process with him and then the next day people were up in arms at the factory.

> Apparently, up to this point, the old hands had assumed that our policy was one of letting the longest serving people go. We had managed to save them through redeployment over a number of years and I guess some goodwill had been generated because of that.

> When they heard about the young chap going this was just something they couldn't seem to accept. I suppose that they could cope with themselves leaving but it somehow symbolised a loss of hope when we had to let go our younger staff.

This episode emphasises how difficult managing change can be, particularly where there are assumptions about 'how things are done around here' which cannot easily be made visible or explicit.

The changes which ICL Logistics have managed to make need to be set against the recessionary environment of the time. David Palk continues:

> The fact that the recession is all around us obviously provides

support for more radical changes to sustain competitiveness. I can see that it would be a lot harder to make these kind of improvements in a more favourable business environment. Our real challenge is to continue to improve through going out there and winning contracts for distribution with other companies — whether it is boom or bust.

The key lessons from this mini-case on ICL Logistics highlight that:

- It is possible to make major improvements in cost competitiveness at the same time as practising a quality culture as a way of life. (ICL Logistics has sought to reduce costs without detriment to quality through simplification and greater people responsiveness.)
- This can be achieved provided that quality management is integral with achieving key business objectives and is well targeted and results-driven. Staff must not confuse 'quality management' with maintaining a cosy, comfortable organisational environment.
- Mobilisation for change comes most effectively through a combination of internally and externally orientated stimuli.
- Change can be mobilised very quickly in a responsive environment. ICL Logistics was 'on the move' in well under six months.

CONCLUSIONS

ICL provides some useful lessons which reinforce those of the Dowty and Prudential cases. These are that:

- quality management, if well targeted, positioned and implemented, can provide a vehicle for driving strategic change successfully forwards;
- but this needs to be integrated with business strategy, business plans and programmes to develop people and processes and rewards and recognition systems;
- through consistency and persistence it can re-shape the paradigm;
- quality management can be pursued (indeed it must be pursued) alongside efforts to improve cost competitiveness, otherwise costs may be managed downwards at the expense of customer value and competitive position.

It will be interesting to see how ICL continues to develop into the mid and late 1990s. Although the external challenges will be formidable, what is certain is that quality management will continue to drive ICL's 'way of life' in steering strategic change.

PART FOUR

STEERING STRATEGIC CHANGE

10

CONCLUSION

INTRODUCTION

We began this book with an ambitious agenda — to explore how strategic change can be implemented more effectively without indulging in prescriptive hype. Although a number of tools and frameworks were used, these were put forward as practical ways of grappling with change rather than as a panacea for all known ills. These tools and frameworks need to be worked on with practice and persistence to yield the results. The spirit underlying this approach is essentially fluid: change may be too complex and uncertain to be programmed precisely — but it can be understood and channelled so as to greatly reduce turbulence and render it manageable.

But tools by themselves are insufficient to implement strategic change effectively. This also requires a shift in the behaviour of people. Ultimately, this shift may require changing the people as well as their culture. This is rarely pain-free and politics-free, and although we look to leadership to make these changes, very often leaders shy away from making these difficult decisions. Paradoxically, these are the very decisions which many individuals in the organisation expect them to make (even those who may suffer as a result).

It may also involve a parallel shift in culture, which has been rediscovered by managers as an important theme in implementing strategic change. Culture is a central means of creating identity within an organisation, of generating commitment and of providing a sense of stability (an island in the sea of turbulent change). It also acts as the medium for sharing understanding about the present and future and filters strategic and tactical decision-making.

As already stated, it may be painful but relatively easy to change key people. It is much harder to shift the organisation's culture. But it may be essential to do this to sustain competitive position and to achieve strategic development.

Attempts at deliberate intervention in organisations to achieve culture shift need to be well orchestrated and sustained. This is borne out in all three cases in this book — Dowty, Prudential and ICL. These interventions need to be realistically targeted — the deeper the intervention the more chance of setting up countervailing forces, and the more skilful the facilitation needs to be.

Interventions also need to be well scoped: limited interventions — for example, team-building or change programmes focusing on one business unit — may achieve temporary shifts which are washed away subsequently by influences in the wider organisation. On the other hand, broad and ambitious change programmes may attempt to 'spread the paint too thinly' with patchy results. You will judge for yourself how successful interventions at Dowty, Prudential and ICL were, but, more importantly, you will need to think through *why* these differences exist — especially in terms of content, process and context, as well as the degree of commitment to change.

It is important to capitalise here on the energies and untapped capability of staff throughout the organisation. Rarely are staff naturally averse to customer care, to achieving profitable growth, to becoming market leader, to achieving excellence in quality. The reason why encounters with some front-line staff in companies (especially in the UK) lead one to conclude that they have just come off a 'hate the customer' programme is probably linked with how staff have been treated themselves over many years.

Many of the perceived 'resistances' which are found in the constraining forces of managers' force field analyses appear due to divisive attitudes and assumptions that people are unwilling to change. Staff are certainly unwilling to change if, as an individual in a major UK company going through a re-structuring put it: 'Management treat us like mushrooms. They keep us in the dark and pour bullshit all over us.' This implies a listening and sensitised approach to managing change which is neverthe-

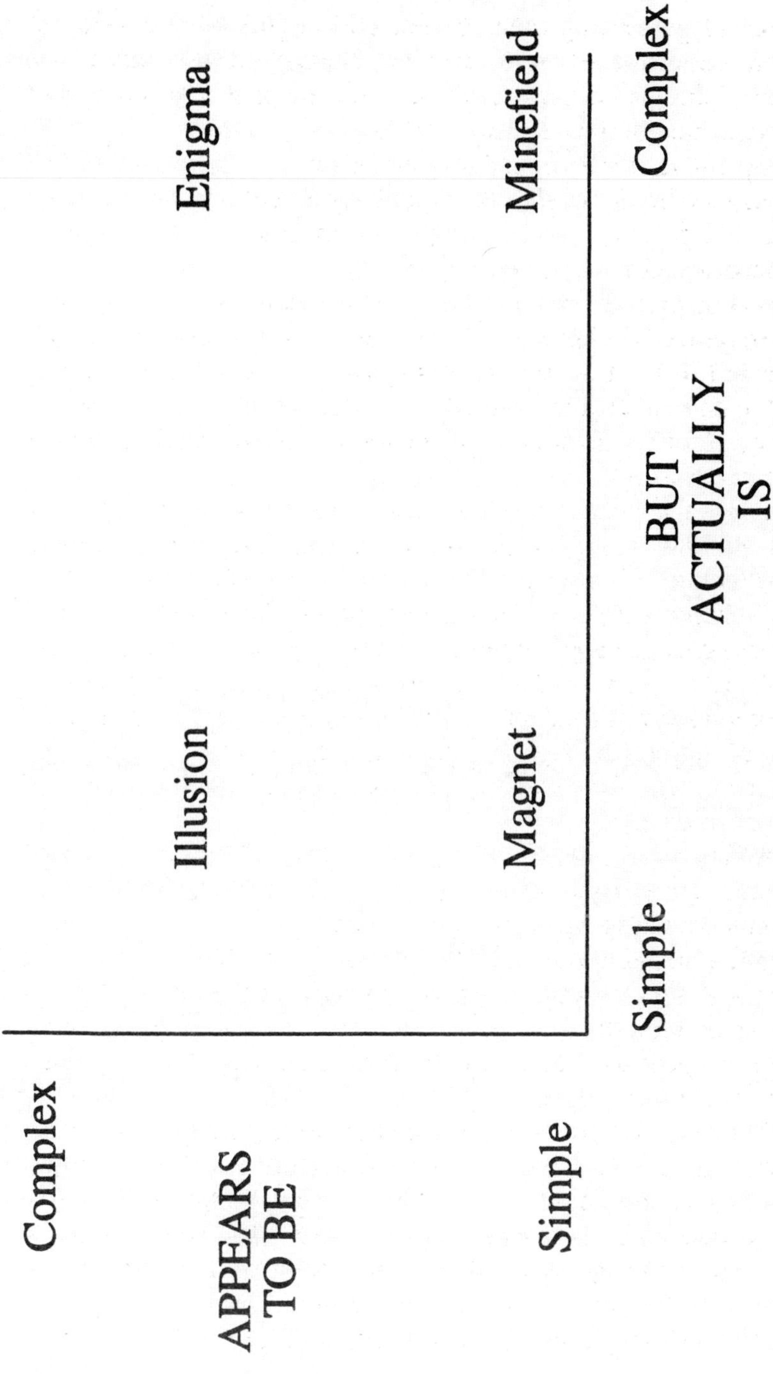

Figure 10.1 Change issue analysis

less consistent with the analytical framework contained in this book.

Here, we need to say a few more words about how the framework and tools can be used in your day-to-day roles.

USING THE TOOLS

In this Guide we have covered a wide range of issues associated with implementing strategic change. Typically, in dealing with change there are issues which:

- may appear to be simple;
- but which may actually be complex;

or

- may appear to be complex;
- but which may actually be simple.

This suggests a framework, as shown in Figure 10.1(on p 199).

Managers who have used the tools in this Guide may find it useful to reflect on how the analysis has gone. This grid shows, for instance, that the 'content' issues of change may appear complex, but in reality may be relatively simple. For instance, an apparently simple issue turned out to be complex in the following cases:

- Dowty Communications: the implementation of the strategic plan.
- Prudential: the structure project — particularly changes to the role of the first line supervisor.
- ICL: shifting to a marketing-led culture.

Equally, instances where an apparently complex issue turned out to be simple were:

- Dowty Communications: whether the company had competitive advantage or whether its position was being eroded.
- Prudential: change was being project-managed but the multitude of projects generated (earlier on in the change) made it more difficult to manage. Key underlying change thrusts were smaller in number.
- ICL: the task of achieving cost competitiveness seemed very difficult until management hit on the notion of bidding for the business from scratch in order to cut free from unnecessary complexity.

Management's attention in implementing change tends to veer onto 'safe territory' issues (in the bottom left-hand box or 'the magnet' — issues which appear simple and actually are simple). Typically, managers nibble at those issues which appear more complex, but are less able to spot where these are essentially 'simple' or 'illusion'. This requires not so much the much-heralded 'strategic vision' but more of a 'simplification vision'. The most dangerous area of all is where managers see something as simple, which is, in reality, very complex ('the minefield') — especially where this involves dealing with changes in the management process or in the paradigm. Where the help of a facilitator is enlisted, managers may well resist attempts to highlight this complexity for fear that the facilitator is on a 'job creation' mission.

This is not to say that complexity is a 'given' — wherever possible it should be reduced. This can be achieved by defining the change objective explicitly and by using project management processes to define results, tasks and resources and timescales.

SHORT EXERCISE

Using Figure 10.1 plot the key change issues which you need to deal with over the next twelve months. How did you originally see these issues (simple or complex, in between)? How do you now see them following analysis of the change process, enabling and constraining forces, stakeholder and paradigm analysis etc?

This brief exercise has highlighted the value of probing change issues to identify where the biggest change minefields may be, and how you can set about moving these around, or dismantling them. But what still remains is to provide a vivid overview of how this book should be used to aid further reflection and action.

The Guide can be used most effectively as follows:

- First, the tool kit should be used to diagnose the 'strategic change issues' faced by the organisation in totality, especially to devise a strategy vision, key thrusts for change and individual change objectives, force field, stakeholder and paradigm analysis.
- It should then be used to address the specific issues within your own personal management role, focusing not merely on short-term issues

('the next six months') but also the longer term (for most managers 'the next two years').

- As a cross-check, you should compare whether the 'management role' issues mesh with those of the wider organisation. Are there issues in the organisation which should or may impact on your role but which you have not taken fully into account?

There may also be agendas for personal strategic change in relating how your own capability fits your role ('what business I am in') — both current and future.

FINAL EXERCISE

What is your current fit with your organisation (in terms of personal strengths and weaknesses versus the demands of your role)? How is your role changing over the next three years, twelve months, etc? What role do you see yourself in in three or more years time? What changes in your skills and style do you need to make to achieve this personal change objective? What enablers and barriers exist in meeting this objective? What action plans will give you a better chance of achieving personal change and development?

So far so good. However, the main barrier to putting these frameworks into practice is the apparent reluctance of most managers to using management tools. This can be seen in the following example:

THE CASE OF THE SHY CHANGE MANAGER

A senior manager of a financial services company recently attended a public programme on 'Managing Change'. Following an 'issue analysis' to brainstorm and then analyse his complex change issues, he then analysed these using both force field analysis and stakeholder analysis. This gave a good 'feel' of where his biggest problems were. His 'action steps' were described as follows: 'The change tools have really highlighted the massive change agenda which I am facing. When I get back to my staff on Monday we will sit down as a team to look together at these issues but I won't be calling it force field analysis, I will have to somehow call it something else.'

The above example is by no means exceptional. A hurdle with using the change tools is the use of a new vocabulary which, however simple, implies some change in mind-set. Here we reach a dilemma, as re-naming the tools, for example as 'change analysis', may dilute the symbolic significance attached to change tools. Alternatively, using the existing labels may send up a 'bow wave' of resistance to change.

But this would not be a problem if the top manager (or managers) in the organisation were to give symbolic approval by using the tools himself. This implies that some involvement at top management level in using change tools and frameworks is a sine qua non of steering strategic change. Going back to the 'top-down' versus 'bottom-up' controversy highlighted in Chapter 1, it suggests a difficult balancing act between initiating top-down change in parallel with bottom-up change.

This might seem an impossible feat — equivalent to the task of building the Channel Tunnel starting at both ends simultaneously, with both British and French teams deciding independently where, when and how they should start. The frameworks for identifying change issues described in this book serve as ways of mapping the change so that there is more than a fighting chance of 'meeting in the middle'.

Chapters 5 and 6 serve as ongoing references in helping you implement strategic change. But checklists on their own will not overcome the political task of setting a strategic vision and of sub-sequently implementing change: this requires considerable deter-mination and sustained effort. Sometimes, the timescales for achieving change goals may appear longer than the commitment and patience currently available. These timescales can sometimes be telescoped, but this is not always possible — on other occasions, the change may resist time compression. Again, a useful device is to set milestones of progress which signify value generated through change. Small successes in the form of achievement of early milestones may be an essential part of relief from the toil.

KEY MESSAGES FOR THE FUTURE

It is said that there are only two certainties in life — death and taxes. We can now add a third — change and how to implement it strategically. This does not mean managing change in a passive way, but constantly challenging and shaping the forces which give birth to change.

With the external and internal business environment in increasing flux, the flipside of uncertainty and change is the need to gain a feeling of 'security' from new sources, particularly from flexibility and capability. 'Flexibility' suggests that the individual, his or her work team and the wider organisation will not collapse because of a sudden bout of discontinuous change. 'Flexibility' also implies potential movement: the individual and his organisation can find new tasks and environments in which to apply his (or 'its') skills. 'Capability' suggests a much richer mix of competencies than has traditionally been found in managers bred primarily in a single function. But faced with intensity of change appearing to strain at flexibility and exceed capability, managers may vote for a return to old sources of security. They may opt to cling to old ways of 'doing things around here'. They will certainly resist initiatives to flatten structures, to remove artificial privileges and trappings of autocratic power. Sometimes, this resistance may manifest itself actively and visibly, and sometimes more deviously through sabotage of change initiatives. Attempts to shift values will inevitably threaten existing power bases and will set up countervailing forces.

Implementing strategic change is, therefore, an intensely political task. Although management may employ tools such as strategic reviews, quality and culture change programmes, restructuring and downsizing, they should be clear and explicit about their objectives and expected outcomes. Programmes for change where the purpose is unclear, implicit or hyped will set up false expectations, which in turn will rebound.

But the external pressure for change will continue to build year on year as the number of markets which have been protected by regulation, national boundaries, government protectionism or cosy industry structures is eroded. The old protective structures are crumbling and there will be no looking back (as did Lot's wife) to 'how nice and cosy it once used to be'.

But, at the same time, this might open up opportunities for organisations able to hold themselves fluid without losing their sense of order and direction. Order and direction will be provided just as much by management software (as illustrated by the management tools in this book) as by traditional hardware (strategic, marketing, financial and operational tools). Being fast, fit and flexible may well turn the fear of implementing strategic change truly into fun, when the failures of the past are avoided.

In order to reinforce the learning lessons of the Guide, you are now invited to participate in the simulation of implementing strategic change

CONCLUSION

in Blackbridge Technology. Remember, your Guide is unfinished until you have worked through Appendix II, where you will play the role of non-executive director during some turbulent times at Blackbridge.

APPENDIX I
LESSONS FROM THE
CHANGE GURUS

INTRODUCTION

This Appendix is a condensed review of what 'change gurus' have contributed to the debate on 'implementing strategic change'. It will be of great help to the manager who wants to learn more about where change frameworks have come from and also for the MBA student. But before we begin to distil the key lessons from the ideas of the change gurus, we need, first, to distinguish between the content of what they say from the style in which the messages are conveyed.

In order to shake the assumptions of their audiences, some change gurus are inclined to be aggressively controversial and to be 'loud' in the way in which they deliver their message. This may alienate certain European audiences and may result in some powerful messages not getting through, as is illustrated in the following example.

EXAMPLE OF CULTURAL BARRIERS TO 'THE CHANGE MESSAGE'

During an MBA programme at a leading UK business school, several Harvard Business School videos were used to deal with a number of change issues, including one featuring Rosabeth Moss Kanter. This video on 'Synergies and New Ventures' figured Rosabeth extolling the virtues of being 'fast, friendly and focused' in a number of 'successful US corporations'. During the video Rosabeth Kanter attacks divisive approaches to management based on internal competition between managers within a corporation. She describes these as being 'cowboy management' and vividly illustrates the downsides of this management style.

This and other messages are delivered in a style which is overpowering to many European managers. After watching the Kanter video, one MBA student reflected:

> I did not dislike the video: there were some good messages. But I went away with my head ringing with confusing and loud voices. I found I just couldn't stand back from the confrontational style and coldly analyse the sound messages which were buried there.

The above example tells us much, not only about the content of the 'change message' and the need for clarity, but also about evangelical change gurus who may over-market their merchandise. Equally, it tells us about the receptiveness of European managers to impassioned pleas to mobilise as collective groups. (Interestingly, two American-born managers in the audience found Rosabeth Kanter's style 'perfectly normal'.)

Coping with 'the hype'

But this incident also highlights that we may not be so good (still) at thinking about 'process'-related issues. It, therefore, reveals how easily an intended communication strategy can backfire or become distorted: simplicity (but not over-simplification) is critical. Second, it highlights how 'the change imperative message' can become a turn-off if it is delivered always with the same, highly prescriptive tone and in an unvarying, blanket-like way. Third, it also highlights how 'the message' is filtered out, not merely by managers' cognitive preconceptions but also by cultural attitudes and values which are more deeply embedded. The 70 MBA students appeared to be governed more by the question 'do I like this person and the way in which she (or he) is talking to me?' rather than 'do I agree that these things make sense?'

Even if the 'change gurus' are 'right', the North American flavour which attaches itself to 'the message' may be a major barrier to our taking any of their ideas on board. Indeed, one of the ingredients for this book — the idea of making it above all a practical guide — came from a member of the culture change team of a major international group, who suggested that European managers are much more likely to 'switch on' by assimilating practical tools rather than exhortations to engage in 'the battle for change'.

Before we look more closely at the messages, it is also worthwhile to point out that there is some element of over-packaging in what certain gurus are seeking to communicate. It is hardly surprising, therefore, that their ideas sometimes have a remarkably short shelf-life. Cynically, one might point to the number of times that a company has been lauded as 'excellent' or 'leading edge' only to be rapidly reappraised as 'running out of ideas', and where its strategic and financial health has become, at best, precarious. In particular, the cases explored in this book are not put forward as examples of wonder and excellence for others to proceed to shoot down. They are realistic accounts of both the opportunities and the problems in the change process.

Despite the attacks which can be levelled at 'the gurus', there is still a very strong case for distilling the key messages from past thinking on change generally in order to produce a practical guide to implementation. This involves extracting 'the best' ideas from the gurus as follows:

- the Prescriptive;
- the Interpretative.

The prescriptive gurus

Introducing the 'Seven S's

The 'prescriptive' school of change gained momentum in the early 1980s principally through the rise of 'excellence' theories. Peters and Waterman's *In Search of Excellence* (1982) rapidly became a management best-seller and did much to open up the market for management books. It described 'excellent management' in a number of major US companies and related this to the 'Seven S's (a McKinsey framework). These stood for:

- strategy;
- structure;
- style;
- staff;

- skills;
- systems;
- shared values.

The merits of this framework were both its simplicity and its ability to encompass the key elements of managing change. The disadvantages were that it does not, in itself, describe how the various elements should interact, nor how to manage an intervention which spans several of these areas in an organisation.

The 'Seven S's remains a useful tool, however, which is discussed earlier. However, the 'shared values' element does seem to be somewhat forced (interestingly, this is the one element which many managers forget, even though it may be critical in implementing strategic change).

The worst is yet to come — dealing with chaos

Encouraged by the success of *In Search of Excellence*, Tom Peters went solo, writing a powerful follow-up book called *Thriving on Chaos* (1987). This selected an underlying issue identified in the previous work — turbulence — and sought to turn 'a problem' into 'an opportunity'. Peters emphasised that there was enjoyment to be had from shaking past organisational certainty with ever increasing waves of change — even where this culminated in apparent (or real) chaos.

In *Thriving on Chaos* Peters presents a clear and comprehensive account of the key areas of transition which a 'more responsive' complex organisation faced into the 1980s and 1990s. The book is, however, overshadowed by the author's presentational style which, like Rosabeth Kanter's, runs the risk of aggravating the barriers towards experimenting with new ideas of proactive change management.

The theme of chaos is an interesting one which has recently become even more central to the change debate. Recent scientific theories that chaos is more prevalent in the world than has previously been thought have spilled over into management theory, and this is now explored.

Building from examples of where micro-level systems change in the natural world (for example a butterfly taking off in one part of the world can ultimately result (through knock-on effects) in a hurricane elsewhere (see Gleick, 1990)), management theorists have begun to challenge the 'ordered' view of the business universe. (On a recent visit to Steven Hawking's laboratory at Cambridge, it was suggested that the universe was no longer considered to be made out of 'particles' but from cylindrical soft tubes with approximate position in space and time — a kind of pasta riddled with holes of uncertainty.)

But these laudable ideas can themselves overplay the role of 'chaos' in the management arena. They may be yet another form of 'corporate valium' which, although it makes managers feel more comfortable, may encourage reactiveness as they believe 'well, it is all ultimately down to chaos'.

The idea of 'chaos' comes from understanding systems in nature which are of a potentially unstable nature. Sometimes, however, a 'change system' within a business can move out of equilibrium quite predictably as a new factor is introduced. This could be, for example, a new leader or a drop in business performance. Sometimes, these factors may aspire to accentuate change and sometimes they may freeze change (for example, the management may draw back from change efforts in order to shore up business performance). But an understanding of context will usually reveal why a change went forward or was stopped. Only in the longer-term does it become much more difficult to predict the outcomes of complex interacting factors (those which Ghemawat (1991) describes as 'wicked complexity') but even more in the longer-term the trend at a macro level may be predictable — at least in terms of clusters of 'possible futures' or scenarios (see, in particular, the case on Blackbridge Technology — in Appendix II).

Flattening the organisation — who will survive?

Moving on from the exciting, but partly unhelpful, theme of chaos, Charles Handy (1989) in the UK has emphasised the revolutionary transformations which were about to reshape companies into flatter, more flexible structures. Specific enablers such as telecommunications and more use of external contractors foreseen by Handy are increasingly being seen as a means of making complex organisations more responsive and cheaper to run in the 1990s. These changes impact on both structure and style. In *The Age of Unreason*, for example, Handy contrasts organisations based on 'pyramid'-type structures (the main model in the 1950s to the 1970s in the Western world) with flatter, leaner and more responsive structures. He also gives us a futuristic vision of a 'clover-leaf' organisation where a cadre of permanent in-house workers are supported by external, specialist sub-contractors.

As at 1992, Handy's vision still seems somewhat futuristic. This is despite the growing army of small businesses and consultancies which have sprung up, particularly in the UK. These developments seem to have been led principally by the 'entrepreneurial culture' in the 1980s (particularly in the UK) and do not necessarily reflect a firm shift towards a large and permanent army of consultancy sub-contractors. Most managers in major companies still see their future as 'within a large company'. Where they are forced into a consultancy role, as a result of restructuring programmes, this is often seen as an interim period 'between jobs' — with one or two exceptions. There seems, therefore, to be a gap between what organisations say they are trying to do (their espoused theory) and what they are actually doing (theory in-use) (Argyris, 1977).

Quick on your feet

Coming back to 'the gurus', we need now to return to Rosabeth Kanter, who was an additional voice emphasising responsiveness and flexibility. Kanter examined practice within a number of (again mainly US) corporations in her weighty book on *The Change Masters* (1983) and also in the sequel *When Giants Learn to Dance* (1989). Again, the important messages about developing strategies for change are buried in a considerable mass of case material, with the result that key messages have to be teased out.

So far, our review may appear to be slightly disappointing. But it is essential to clear away the clutter before building a practical framework which will allow the reader to implement strategic change more effectively.

Turning up the heat — a love of contention

If we move on to the late 1980s, further themes emerge. Pascale's book *Managing on the Edge* (1990) emphasises the use of 'contention' as a force to drive change. This emphasises some of the 'harder' forces at work in the change process — as opposed to those which revert to organisational values. Although there is plenty of merit in Pascale's message, we are in danger of making a particular virtue into a 'total approach' to implementing strategic change. Pascale does, however, provide a counterweight to earlier prescriptions (coming more from the 'culture-led' school) that providing the underlying processes for change are in place, then organisations will move forward of their own volition.

More recently, the theme of 'forcing change through by tangible measures' has been taken up by Beer et al (1990). They highlight that a crucial ingredient involves altering some of the tangible structures, controls and practices within the organisation. They argue that, by shaking or shifting the tangible fabric of the organisation, new behaviour patterns will emerge and these, in turn, will generate new underlying attitudes. The underlying theory here is not new: in social psychology it was highlighted several decades ago that if individuals enter into new forms of role behaviour, their underlying attitudes will experience a shift to minimise 'dissonance'. Readers trained in psychology will recognise this as the theory of 'cognitive dissonance'.

Beer et al's thinking adds an important reminder to those contemplating major change primarily through 'softer' initiatives — for example 'cultural change' or 'total quality management'. It also emphasises that many centrally-co-ordinated change initiatives fail for a variety of reasons — the diversity in local contexts (including culture), the difficulties of sustaining fundamental change throughout a large organisation simultaneously, and also because of 'ownership issues'. On the other hand, their argument that 'local initiatives' are 'the most effective way forward' may be inappropriate for managing certain kinds of change — for example, in quality management (having 'zero defects' does mean that you only have to have these in certain centres of high quality, whilst pockets of poor quality can be tolerated). Again, Beer et al's views fall into the more aggressive 'hard' school of implementing strategic change.

Simple is beautiful

Notable cases of well-publicised change have recently added impetus to the debate. In the US, Welch's (1989) account of change at General Electric emphasised the virtues of simplification and also of decisions in implementing strategic change ('self-confidence'). Other examples of organisations striving to be flexible and externally-focused include (in the 1980s) British Airways and (in the 1990s) BP in the UK. It has become more fashionable for larger companies to focus on fundamental change by calling it, for example, 'Project 1990' (at BP), or 'Project Sovereign' (at BT), both of which mixed the 'culture-led' school with the 'hard' school of change.

Around all of these major efforts at organisational transformation you will find a number of commentators: the catalysts who exaggerate progress and achievements and who are inclined to downplay or deny failures or partial success. Equally, there are the many cynics both internally within the organisation and externally who, for real or imaginary reasons, wish to snipe at efforts to implement change.

The rise of the new ritual of change

Turning back to the gurus, an important contribution to this debate is from Schaffer and Thomson (1992) who argue that change programmes have become new rituals which lack business focus. Drawing on illustrations from a number of companies, they draw attention to the failure to reap the benefits of change, for example through quality programmes. This appears to be due, in part, to a 'blunderbuss' approach — firing at particular change issues, yet not building in sufficient milestones and feedback so that the change process becomes a genuinely open learning experience.

Schaffer and Thomson's argument is very much a reflection of management processes being badly implemented. If we accept that this is as common as their research suggests, there is perhaps a strong case for anchoring change programmes primarily in tangible and targeted results. But however refreshing Schaffer and Thomson are in pointing out the importance of content in directing change, it is essential not to overplay this argument which comes from the 'hard school' of change. Although Schaffer and Thomson do emphasise the importance of strategic or holistic vision, in practice their path to mobilisation involves incremental roll-out, with the attendant problems of fragmentation. Managers' 'vision' may not be so robust as to remain whole whilst their change activities are structured in a way which dictates fragmentation.

What does it all add up to?

The key lessons which we can therefore distil from the prescriptive change gurus are that:

- Strategic change is many-faceted and requires managing a number of areas of change at the same time (and is a corporate juggling act).
- Traditional hierarchies are becoming increasingly less relevant in complex companies. Companies operating primarily through hierarchy are likely to lose competitiveness in a business environment where the pace of change is increasing, where there is major external uncertainty and where customers require faster and more appropriate response to their needs.
- Besides the 'softer' areas (such as 'shared values'), implementing strategic change may necessitate intervention in tangible structures,

changes in staff and radical changes in systems. It may also require the use of contention and deliberate challenge in order to establish a 'constructive tension' in the organisation.

- Change programmes may need to be focused on tackling specific business issues, as well as being seen purely as doing good things generally — it may be helpful to have, in part, a 'results focus', as long as this does not become overburdened with measurement and control.

- The issue of capability to implement strategic change has a major bearing on competitive advantage and (with time lags) on financial performance.

The interpretative gurus

Managing change in fragments

It is worthwhile taking the linkage between capability to implement change and competitive advantage a stage further. Let us now incorporate the views of theorists who highlight the importance of understanding how the implementation process actually works, as opposed to prescribing how it ought to work. Here, we see some useful inputs from the 'process' school of strategic management. For example, Quinn (1980) argued that strategic change may unfold as an evolutionary, rather than a revolutionary, process. He linked this with the idea of 'incremental' strategic development. He observed that in a number of major companies strategic decisions were rarely made as part of some holistic 'grand-plan', but appeared to have been taken largely as 'add-ons' to the existing core strategy.

In order to emphasise that this 'incrementalism' was not 'a-rational' he called this 'logical incrementalism' — in other words, that incremental thinking had a logic within its own, albeit narrow, context. This contrasts sharply with the more 'analytical' school of strategy whose most complete manifestation is found in Porter's work (1985) which is often characterised as the 'design school' of strategic management.

A 'watch this space' view of strategic change

Quinn's insights were reinforced by Mintzberg (1978) who highlighted the importance of 'emergent' (as opposed to 'deliberate' strategy). Mintzberg argued that the path of strategic change may only emerge as a pattern with hindsight. The shifts in direction are thus evident only by historical analysis of the links in the various 'logics' of change. In addition, the core strategy may typically be 'fuzzy' and thus capable of divergent interpretations by managers.

Mintzberg's account of strategic development appears much more plausible as a descriptive account of how new strategy is formulated. Recent work by Johnson (1992) shows how organisations can move through periods of particularly turbulent or discontinuous change and then stabilise on a more 'incremental footing' (see, particularly, Chapter 7 on Dowty Communications in this book) which is echoed by Grundy and King (1992) in the same edition of *Long Range Planning*).

The power and pitfalls of organisational learning

In many of these interpretative accounts of strategic change, the adaptive and learning elements come to the fore either implicitly or explicitly. For instance, Ansoff (1982) identifies the importance of learning within strategic planning for change, especially to create what he calls a 'platform' of shared understanding and skills for implementation. Garratt (1990) also suggests that this can and should be formalised in the idea of a learning organisation, a theme which is also echoed by Senge (1990). The message coming through strongly from these sources is that implementing strategic change is inseparable from organisational learning , thus notions of any 'quick fix' to change problems from more prescriptive gurus are misplaced.

But an important caveat to bear in mind here is that organisations are notoriously bad at learning — except where this is of a simple and routine nature. Where an organisation is implementing strategic change, the learning processes will inevitably be complex (or 'double loop' — Argyris, 1977, 1991). Strategic insights are then likely to be quickly lost as the organisation reverts to its past mind-set.

More ambitious attempts have been made to trace the process of implementing strategic change and to relate this to shifts in competitive advantage. As an interpretative account, this task is of monumental proportions as a recent book by Pettigrew and Whipp (1991) shows. But theorists appear caught between suggesting highly simplistic models and of muddying the picture with over-complex empirical analysis. For instance, after an impressive, multi-perspective view of strategic change, Pettigrew and Whipp conclude that a relatively small number of factors are crucial. Of particular importance to us here are 'maintaining coherence' and being able to link 'strategy' to operations — in other words, overcoming the perils of incrementalism and of 'strategy' being swept off course by unpredictable forces.

Making sense of the realists

The lessons from the interpretative and realist theories of change are therefore that:

- A more 'normal' or common mode of managing change is characteristically one where strategic change is managed incrementally rather than 'holistically'. Also, the path of change is influenced considerably with 'emergent' and 'unintended' as opposed to 'deliberate' strategies. Even the 'core strategy' is often fuzzy.
- Highly prescriptive approaches to implementing strategic change cut across managers' practical behaviour.
- Although there are links between the capability of implementing strategic change and competitive performance, it is exceedingly difficult to understand precisely how these linkages operate and with what effect. It must, therefore, be even harder to manage these.

In summary, change gurus and theorists present us with a picture which is at once helpful and also unhelpful. On the one hand, they alerted us to the pressure for achieving major shifts in how organisations operate and compete. But many of their 'model companies' have failed to sustain excellence in implementing change — particularly when the going gets tough. They have fallen foul themselves of the process of change. Also, their prescriptive messages appear single sided, overblown or naive when considering how to remove the barriers to change.

Equally, the 'interpretative' theorists appear stuck in exploratory accounts of change and unwilling to put forward practical recommendations for implementing strategic change for fear of being labelled 'guru-esque'. In some ways, one has more sympathy as these theorists are trying hard to understand what is actually going on in the change process before any frameworks which may be used on an applied basis emerge.

This book sought to achieve a balance between seeking to understand 'what is going on' which makes implementing strategic change such a major problem, whilst drawing out the practical implications for managing this change more effectively. To avoid the worst of both worlds, it is necessary to carve out a 'pluralistic' and practical framework of change, which has been the aim of this Guide.

APPENDIX II
BLACKBRIDGE TECHNOLOGY

OVERVIEW

This appendix describes a company which goes through a number of phases of strategic change. The case study begins in 1983 when the company — Blackbridge Technology — was founded. The names of the company and of all individuals are fictitious.

The purpose of this case simulation is to bring together the tools and techniques and the lessons on implementing strategic change which have been distilled from the first two parts of this book. This is done in a 'safe environment' but you should treat this case as if it were real.

You are invited to complete a number of exercises to practise the tools, which can then be compared with my own 'best view' of the problem. There is no 'right answer', but there will certainly be some analyses which have greater 'fit' than others.

The case can be used as an individual or as a group exercise in order to practise the approaches to implementing strategic change described earlier in the book.

IMPLEMENTING STRATEGIC CHANGE — CASE SIMULATION — BLACKBRIDGE TECHNOLOGY

Introduction

Blackbridge Technology is a relatively successful, medium sized technology group based near the red-brick town of Stonebury within the London-Oxford-Reading triangle. Current sales are £180 million, and the group is looking forward to continued expansion in spite of the recession of the early 1990s. This case is derived from interviews with a non-executive director of Blackbridge who invites you to share in his dilemmas of strategic change.

The case begins by describing the history and current context of Blackbridge Technology, before going on to analyse the effects of changes in strategy, structure and culture. This leads on to an evaluation of current position and capability and future ambitions and intent, before moving on to implementation issues. It ends by raising a number of key questions on implementing strategic change at Blackbridge.

There are two key questions you should consider throughout:

- Do you believe that Blackbridge's management fully addressed the external and internal implications of strategic change in their plans at each stage?
- If not, what further actions do you believe should have been taken to forge a more coherent and robust implementation plan?

History and context

Blackbridge Technology was founded in the UK in 1983 by an entrepreneur, Sam Wheeze. Originally an electronics engineer, Sam Wheeze worked for ten years in a major electronics group, Electroclamp plc, before spotting a new market opportunity for a product called SUPERSWITCH in 1982. This product enabled computer networks to interface more efficiently by eliminating errors in initial and final transmission of data. These errors might occur at particularly high transmission speeds.

Sam sought to interest his superiors at Electroclamp in SUPERSWITCH opportunity but after numerous attempts to force this innovation through the rather rigid doors of senior management's attention, he decided to admit defeat.

In 1982, Sam Wheeze went into partnership with a rich friend, Bill Flood, who was able to put up the initial capital for a new venture. From the start, Blackbridge Technology was a commercial success. Sam Wheeze's new product SUPERSWITCH proved to be very powerful in linking two technology streams (hence the 'bridge' element of the Blackbridge name). It was also able to do this without visibly changing the larger electronics system of which it was a part (hence the 'black' element of the Blackbridge name — it was 'invisible' to the user).

The SUPERSWITCH technology was patented and was relatively invulnerable to imitation through technical substitutes — at least in the earlier years. In those early days, the critical success factors for achieving competitive advantage for Blackbridge were to:

- establish a clear image in the market place for both SUPERSWITCH and for Blackbridge as a credible supplier to major electronics companies and to government bodies;
- achieve adequate (but not superior) quality levels;
- satisfy demand which grew very rapidly;
- tap into sufficient sources of finance in order to sustain rapid growth;
- expand the organisation to keep pace with rapid growth.

Figure App II.1 gives a graphic picture of the growth in turnover (and profitability) of Blackbridge Technology from 1983 to 1987

	1983 £m	1984 £m	1985 £m	1986 £m	1987 £m
Turnover	0.5	2.2	7.5	15.8	24.2
Profitability	0.1	0.5	1.8	3.2	4.9
Profitability %	20%	23%	24%	20%	20%
Employees	10	22	52	85	115

Note: profits are before taxation.

Figure App II.1   Blackbridge Technology — financial results in early years

The 'dash for growth' was made in order to secure a position of market leader in this niche before competition (possibly from Far Eastern sources) appeared on the scene.

The first five years were marked with great enthusiasm and mind-set which clearly reflected the assumption that Blackbridge was unbeatable. The success of SUPERSWITCH was followed by related innovation so that a whole family of related switches were created. At that time, most of the sales were to the UK but increasingly Blackbridge began to penetrate both the US and Europe via export sales.

Although Blackbridge was able to recruit a relatively strong management team during 1983-84 (for a company of its size), by 1985-86 the sheer rate of growth began to give rise to some strains. By then, Bill Flood had retired from the scene and Blackbridge was steered (on a tactical basis) by a triad of:

Chief Executive:	Sam Wheeze
Operations Director:	Mike Lamb
Financial Director:	Dick Slaughter

Based on the excellent (reported) results of 1986, in 1987 40 per cent of the company was floated on the Unlisted Securities Market (USM) providing major new funds for expansion. As part of this exercise the top management team was strengthened by two new directors:

Sales Director:	Jim Brand
Personnel Director:	Mary Morbid

Jim Brand had previously worked as a sales director in a (failed) computer company which had been wiped out by cheap Japanese imports. Mary Morbid was recruited from a UK retailer where she had previously been personnel manager of a major London store. (Although an apparently curious choice, Mary was well thought of in her previous role as a strong, independent individual. It had also proven difficult to recruit from within the industry for the kind of package which Blackbridge felt it could afford — Dick Slaughter set the parameters for this package.)

Following these management changes it was also made explicit within the stock market flotation document that a new managing director would be sought with prior experience of running a technology-based division with over £50m turnover. This would enable Sam Wheeze to spend more time dealing with external stakeholders and steering new product innovation (a kind of joint Chairman/Director of Product Development role). It was agreed that this would be the best place for Sam's entrepreneurial talents.

Following these changes, Blackbridge continued to make progress in its core activities, although in 1988 results were marred by an exceptional loss within a recent acquisition in Spain of £2 million (this was Blackbridge's first major acquisition). Over the next five years Blackbridge's results (again with profits before tax) were:

	1988 £m	1989 £m	1990 £m	1991 £m	1992 £m
Turnover	32.1	47.5	69.4	105.9	181.0**
Profitability	7.4	9.1	11.9	17.4	29.1
Extraordinary items	<2.0>				
Profitability %*	23%	19%	17%	16%	16%
Employees	140	190	240	310	620

* before extraordinary item
** of which £35m was a new acquisition

The 1992 figure for turnover was inflated by the major acquisition of a UK software company, Megathink, for £52m. Based in a country house in Hampshire, Megathink contributed in 1992 to £35m of Blackbridge Group's turnover and £6m of post-tax profits. Megathink employed a staff of 270. The acquisition was relatively cheap, as by 1992 the software industry was out of favour generally in the UK stock market.

The acquisition was partly funded by a rights issue by Blackbridge, whose rapid growth in earnings provided an attractive base for raising additional capital. The offer was part cash and part 'paper for paper' — a feat which was manageable because of Blackbridge's track record of fast and profitable growth.

The 1992 performance of Blackbridge's core business was still an outstanding achievement, coming as it did in the middle of a recession. Demand for Blackbridge's products grew as it enabled the cost and effectiveness of existing as well as new networks to be reduced.

The objectives behind the acquisition of Megathink were:

- to achieve a better balance of activities between hardware-based products and software-based products;

- to exploit Megathink's profile and contacts with major European companies in the electronics and defence industries;
- to acquire management skills: both the Chief Executive of Megathink, Dan Doom, and its Managing Director, Mark Moan, were extremely knowledgeable of their industry and also had extensive contact with customers of Blackbridge's core products.

Question 1

From what you now know of the origins of Blackbridge Technology, what do you see as being the key internal challenges likely to be faced by the newly combined group? (You may choose to do a force field analysis to explore the feasibility of the following change objective: 'To integrate Blackbridge and Megathink with maximum benefit and with least disruption and cost.')

Strategy, structure and culture

Prior to 1992, Blackbridge Technology had followed a 'strategy' which was relatively loose and entrepreneurial. Much of 'the strategy' was in the head of Sam Wheeze, although in latter years the financial director, Dick Slaughter, had instigated a three-year (mainly financial) plan. This was triggered primarily because of the need for successive flotations of Blackbridge's shares.

By 1992, the need for a more concrete framework for becoming more strategic was beginning to become apparent as Blackbridge Technology Group (henceforward known as 'BTG') had become more complex to manage. It was also intended to continue the growth in activities mainly by organic development in order to a) avoid loss of focus, and b) to enable the Megathink acquisition to be digested (although smaller acquisitions were not being ruled out).

Prior to 1992 Blackbridge had thus been growing (primarily organically) at rates of between 40 per cent and 80 per cent per annum. This had been achieved primarily through a relatively flat structure, although in recent years further tiers of management had begun to appear. Sam Wheeze and his directors were concerned to avoid a 'creeping bureaucracy' which would stifle the company's entrepreneurial culture.

Following the acquisition of Megathink (which was presented as a 'merger' to the staff of both companies), one of the main issues was how to structure the new group to 'bring in' key management from Megathink and exploit synergies without producing a monolithic organisation. This raised issues about *both* structure and culture.

The Directors of Blackbridge Technology had seen 'the culture' of Megathink as being relatively similar to their own, with the exception that Megathink staff appeared to be more obsessed with 'technically perfect solutions' and less bothered about 'going aggressively for growth'. Prior to the acquisition Megathink had grown at a more modest rate of 15-20% and had virtually 'stood-still' in the depths of the 1990-92 recession.

Despite the vague concerns about 'culture differences' of his fellow directors, especially Mary Morbid, Personnel Director, Sam Wheeze was primarily worried about structure. A secondary issue was the longer-term strategy which Sam felt could be handled initially by establishing a concise 'mission'. Third came the issue of culture which Sam felt would more or less resolve itself over time through gradually increasing co-working between Blackbridge and Megathink's staff.

The new structure which emerged was a hybrid one. The management team of Blackbridge Technology itself was retained, whilst a new group board was established. This reflected the following positions:

Chairman/CEO, Blackbridge:	Sam Wheeze
Deputy Chairman/CEO Megathink:	Dan Doom
Financial Director:	Dick Slaughter
Group Operations Director:	Mike Lamb
Director of Strategic Planning:	Mark Moan

Question 2

Do you believe that Sam Wheeze has fully understood the needs of Blackbridge Technology in prioritising areas for change — particularly in his choice to focus on (in order of priority) structure, strategy and only then on culture?

In addition (and now comes the surprise), the Board has invited you personally — the reader — to become a non- executive Director of BTG plc, following your interest to date in implementing strategic change.

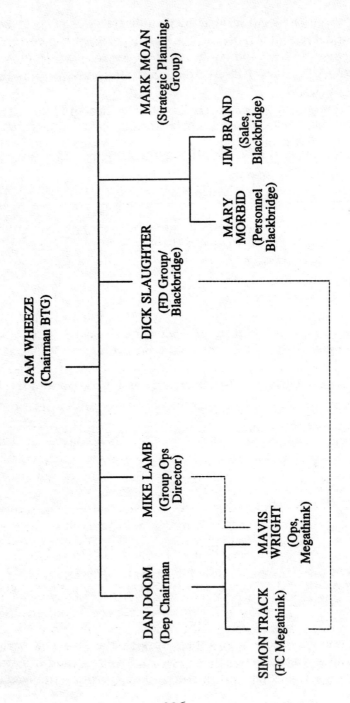

Figure App II.2   Blackbridge Technology Group — structure

You will play an important role in advising BTG over the next five years.

Naturally, there have been some 'losers' in this new structure. Mary Morbid was disappointed not to become group personnel director. Jim Brand was also slightly bitter not to have been appointed director of strategic planning.

The full reporting structure is shown in Figure App II.2.

Current position and capability

Based on your advice that a clear strategy is required for the new group, in early 1993 Sam Wheeze decides to call an 'away day' for senior members of the group. This is held at the secluded country house, Vision Hall, in rural Hampshire. In attendance is yourself, the main board members of BTG and directors of both Blackbridge and Megathink. Outside the main board. Megathink directors not in Blackbridge's board include:

Financial Director, Megathink:	Simon Track
Operations Director, Megathink:	Mavis Wright

This puts the total away-day team at ten people including Mary Morbid, Jim Brand and yourself.

As the team arrive in a sporadic flow of BMWs and SAABs and Japanese Porche lookalikes, it becomes evident that a number of the senior team appear to be unusually nervous as they chink their coffee cups. This is not helped much by Sam Wheeze's heavy assertiveness at the beginning that he is concerned the 'Blackbridge Group is becoming complacent and people are beginning to leave the office before 7 pm'.

The purpose of this away day is to establish current position and capability of the organisation by means of a competitive 'strengths and weaknesses, opportunities and threats (or SWOT) analysis'. The 'SWOT' analysis came out in a great flurry of activity, so that by mid to late morning all of the team were feeling very happy with their output. Further progress is, however, inhibited by the long lunch which Vision Hall catering staff insisted on laying on — smoked salmon and quails eggs, followed by roast beef (from what seems to be half a cow).

This SWOT analysis appears much richer in terms of its internal perceptions of Blackbridge than of its external competitive position — the top team lack sufficiently 'hard' data to perform robust positioning compared to competitors. It is agreed that 'this needs some further looking into'.

The competitive SWOT analysis reveals a number of major issues as follows:

- There appears a good deal of internal confusion about 'who does what' in the new structure, especially between Blackbridge corporate staff and staff in Megathink.
- There is evidence of pronounced culture clash in a number of areas — symptoms of this have arisen in implementing new terms and conditions (especially company car schemes) and in the approach to be taken by joint Blackbridge/Megathink task forces in bidding for large and complex joint projects.
- Concerns about the achievability of ambitious growth targets (as envisaged by Sam Wheeze) have emerged.
- In Blackbridge itself there are important issues concerning the quality of a number of its products.
- The original market position of the SUPERSWITCH product range is under increasing competitive attack and margins are declining, albeit slowly at present.
- At Megathink some key staff (crucial to maintaining the existing business) have voiced that they might consider leaving. In this industry it is not uncommon to find this happening and former staff setting up in competition.
- There are also fears that BTG's standing in financial markets is being downgraded.

Question 3

As non-executive director (newly appointed), you are concerned about these major symptoms of malaise. But at present, you have limited evidence of how fundamental these problems are. Although you have established some credibility with the top team you fear that a direct attack on these issues may be premature. On the other hand, you may miss a vital opportunity to open up a crucial debate. Bearing this in mind, do you think that you should intervene:

a) directly and forcefully during the away day?
b) in a more indirect and less threatening way during the away day?
c) only later, in a private meeting with Sam Wheeze after the 'away day'?

Moving on — Future ambitions and capability

In the event, you decided not to voice direct or indirect questions on the day, but subsequently you intervene in earnest in a private meeting with Sam Wheeze and Dan Doom. Sam responds by suggesting that if he had worried continually about having a 'bomb-proof' organisation, BTG would not occupy its current position. Sam appeared to recognise some of the failings which had been highlighted, but preferred to address these later once a clear agreement on future ambitions (the 'strategic vision') had been reached. Dan Doom appeared quiet and not willing to reveal his position.

You begin to feel that Dan Doom has secret reservations about the current path of strategic change. You also feel that he would do 'a better job' in steering BTG to future success than Sam Wheeze, who seems to be acting as if his role is unchanged, despite the official line that he will becoming less 'hands-on'. From the outside it seems like a clear pattern is emerging of 'growing pains' in the organisation which have gone unrecognised for some time. Although you see this clearly, you believe that management within Blackbridge only realise this dimly, and where they do, they may not rush to admit it.

It is agreed that a second away day will be held and you insist that an external facilitator is employed. Fortunately, Dan Doom proposes a chap called Malcolm Magic who specialises in 'strategic turnarounds', whom he met at a management conference in Brussels. (Malcolm Magic is unusual in that, although he originally is an accountant by training, he works intensively with companies to kindle longer-term organisational change through internal and external analysis.)

Because of the shortage of time, the agenda for the second away day is already set before Malcolm can provide input to designing the process. Also, as Sam is hesitant about using Malcolm he is introduced as an 'external observer who we might well use as a facilitator', rather than as someone who will be 'with us for the entire journey'.

Despite this ambiguity, the second away day goes well — at least in delivering the outputs which were on Sam's agenda. These included:

- A decision to aim to grow organically at an annual rate of 25 per cent over the next four years. This would mean turnover at two and a half times current levels or around £440 million. Although modest by BTG's historical standards, this rate of expansion reflects slower growth in Blackbridge's core business and also the lags in recruiting and developing software staff at Megathink. These moderations to Sam Wheeze's original plans (to grow organically at a compound 40 per cent rate) are suggested by Malcolm Magic who warns that such a high growth rate would be impossible to digest. A 40 per cent rate would mean doubling each two years to reach £700m turnover. Simon Track (group finance director) is 'cautiously optimistic' — probably the best that can be hoped for from an accountant — that this growth rate can be funded with new equity issues and some longer-term debt.

- The projected growth is anticipated primarily from European markets and from existing product and technology base, although no detailed breakdown by country or product or service line over time is laid down.

A decision is taken to run a number of further workshops to devise a more detailed strategy to implement this 'strategic intent'.

Question 4

From what you have been told, do you believe that this 'strategic intent' is a helpful or perhaps an unhelpful guide to further strategic thinking by the top team at BTG?

Implementation issues — diagnosis

One of your own contributions to the second away day is to insist that further and much more detailed work is done to ensure that BTG has a sound enough competitive platform for growth. By coincidence, the day before the second away day, you read in the *Financial Times* how a non-executive director of a leading cleaning services company had experienced misgivings about a company's strategy elsewhere, yet had failed to make his concerns known in a sufficiently timely and vociferous fashion. You wonder whether BTG might well fall into a similar trap of 'going for more growth' when external markets are toughening up and its competitive position is deteriorating slowly but inexorably.

By this stage you have persuaded Sam Wheeze to use Malcolm Magic as a facilitator to steer the thinking process about BTG's future. You feel that Malcolm is absolutely right for the job. However, as Malcolm has other client commitments there may be difficulties in ensuring that he is available at the right time. The following question occurs to you as being important, as you do not believe that the internal management team (even with your input) can mobilise for change. It seems this needs a major shake-up of its 'mind-set'.

Question 5

Do you suggest to Sam Wheeze that Malcolm Magic should be retained formally on a basis of five days per month over the next six months (remember his daily fee rate is £800) or should the team muddle through?

During the first 'strategy implementation' workshop it becomes clear that the platform for future (profitable) growth may be a lot shakier than Sam Wheeze's original vision suggested. In order to fulfil BTG's strategic intent a number of major changes needed to be digested. Malcolm Magic put this powerfully in the following 'change equation':

> Total Change Requirement = (Change to sustain competitive position of Blackbridge's core business)
> *plus*
> (Changes to integrate key elements of Megathink into Blackbridge)
> *plus*
> (Changes to give BTG group an international focus and culture)
> *plus*
> (Future changes required in order to digest further organic growth at a target rate of 25% per annum).

BTG's top team sits quietly as they digest the enormity of change which their past actions and strategic intent pose for them as a team.

Question 6

As a non-executive director, do you believe that you should reinforce or amplify Malcolm's message or do you believe that Malcolm Magic's shock tactics should be left to 'speak for themselves'?

In the event, the top team decides to investigate the severity of these issues in greater depth prior to the next workshop. Each of the above issues is parcelled out to pairs of managers from Blackbridge's top team who have the task of reporting back in three weeks' time. This is structured as follows:

- improving competitive position (existing businesses) — Mark Moan, Mavis Wright;
- Megathink integration — Sam Wheeze, Dick Slaughter;
- international focus and culture — Mary Morbid, Dan Doom;
- evaluating strategic opportunity (newer business areas) — Jim Brand, Simon Track.

Implementation issues — planning

Over the next three weeks, the four pairs of managers went into hyperdrive to explore the issues, with further input by Malcolm Magic. A number of inputs are made ready for the second strategy implementation workshop, namely:

- an overview of target markets and existing competitive position analysed by strategic business area (by product/service/territory);
- a view of turnover and profit (broadly pictured) based on a) a 'realistic' view, and b) a 'pessimistic' view;
- costs of change and the amount of investment required to enable growth to happen and competitive position to be protected;
- a number of specific change thrusts which will enable desired growth and change to happen;
- for each change thrust a force field analysis representing the enablers and barriers to achieving desired change.

During the second strategy implementation workshop, the day is split between four areas, as follows:

Morning
- improving Blackbridge's competitive position;
- integration and synergies with Megathink;

Afternoon
- creating an international company — BTG;
- problems of digesting new growth — organisational structure and people issues.

This agenda proves to be an extremely full day. In fact, the day ends at 9 pm as three hours are spent debating whether and how these changes can be integrated in a coherent whole. Each linkage is painstakingly documented so that subsequent to the workshop Sam Wheeze (helped by Malcolm Magic) can distil a 'Strategic Change Plan'.

At 8.30 pm on this second workshop you raise the point that:

> Well, we seem to have come a long way in a short time but one thing still worries me a bit. What we haven't done is involve your senior managers to both test out the plan and also — by the way — to begin to own it. Even if the plan is the most sensible thing since you launched SUPERSWITCH, Sam, we may be missing a trick here in not involving your implementors.

Although Malcolm Magic quickly whipped in to reinforce this argument, Sam Wheeze responds stonily by saying:

> Look, if we went all around the houses to get everyone's quids-in, we would get a hundred and one strategic visions. I really think we have to drive this one through.

You have visions of Sam Wheeze in a Landrover getting rather stuck in a quagmire but furiously trying to move forward, but there seems little point in continuing this line of argument — Sam seems fixed on restricting strategy formulation to the inner core of top management.

You also notice that Dan Doom, deputy chairman, is looking uncomfortable about this chain of events, and even Mary Morbid, who is usually swayed along by Sam Wheeze's personal charisma and drive, looks ill at ease.

Question 7

Do you believe that you are just becoming a little neurotic or is Sam Wheeze's stubbornness a symptom of some deeper malaise?

Key questions on implementing strategic change

At this juncture, it may be useful to examine a number of possible scenarios of the future for Blackbridge Technology Group — which one do you favour being the most plausible?

Scenario 1: Competitive Success

BTG succeeds in both turning around existing operations and exceeding its growth ambitions. Following the stagnant market conditions of 1990-92, in 1993 a pronounced pick-up is felt in key markets in the industry and BTG sustains a high growth rate to retain its market share. The company's competitive position is improved by concerted measures to improve product and service performance under the new management team. Staff from Blackbridge and Megathink increasingly work in collaborative teams to exploit opportunities of increasing size and complexity in an entrepreneurial and professional fashion.

Financial Performance

	1993 £m	1994 £m	1995 £m	1996 £m
Turnover	215	274	369	443
Profitability	34	52	71	84
Profitability %	16%	19%	19%	19%
Employees	420	491	620	715

Scenario 2: Continued Decline

BTG fails to meet its growth ambitions. Although market conditions recover (as in Scenario 1), BTG loses market share to its main rivals. The turnaround in its products and services takes a lot longer to take effect and it is only by 1995 that major benefits are felt. The time lag for improvement resulted from a number of factors:

- The top team showed uneven commitment to pushing through the measures required for successful change.
- The adverse effects of differing cultures between Blackbridge and Megathink had been severely underestimated.
- A number of problems in its international business outside the UK had developed — these were, in turn, a reflection of weak management and a parochial, national culture.
- Competitors had proved to be increasingly nimble and had continued to open a 'performance gap' with BTG throughout 1993 and the first part of 1994.

Financial Performance

	1993 £m	1994 £m	1995 £m	1996 £m
Turnover	208	237	281	362
Profitability	22	28	42	61
Profitability %	10%	12%	18%	17%
Employees	380	410	445	570

Scenario 3: Nosedive and Turnaround

Although to some extent economic growth resumed in 1993, this was extremely weak owing to an overhang of debt and overcapacity in many Western industries in the 1980s. Instead of increasing economic activity, the Eastern economies (former Soviet Block) stagger from crisis to crisis and Western inward investments to the region pass into a 'black hole'.

In the electronics and related software industry the heady growth of the 1970s and 1980s is not repeated as companies become more discerning about the benefits of new electronic data systems (over and above what they already have).

The market becomes fiercely competitive and mid-range players like BTG are increasingly under squeeze. In 1994-95 there are a number of acquisitions and re-groupings in the industry and two middle-sized players go into receivership.

Not only is BTG fighting on one external front, but there are major internal problems too. In common with Scenario 2, a number of factors conspire to make the turnaround plans to 1994 ineffective and in late 1994 Sam Wheeze is ousted in a boardroom coup. Dan Doom finally loses patience with Sam's optimistic visioning and urging to return to 'the days when we were cut and thrust'. Mary Morbid — who has since gained a seat on BTG's board through her dogged efforts to procure team-working between Blackbridge and Megathink — insists that new blood is required. Dan Doom is made chairman and a new managing director, Tom Barron, is appointed in early 1995 to push through sweeping changes throughout BTG.

Tom Baron is an unusual character. After qualifying as a chartered accountant he was thrown out of the Institute for 'cold calling' and, using his FCA to symbolise being a 'former chartered accountant', began a career as a financial turnaround manager. Tom is given a two-year contract to 'shake the profit out of BTG' after which he will, no doubt, go on to bigger things or retire on his performance bonus.

To see the effects of these changes let us take the performance data one year further at:

Financial performance

	1993 £m	1994 £m	1995 £m	1996 £m	1997 £m
Turnover	189	205	210	270	380
Profitability	18	9	24	45	66
Profitability %	9%	4%	11%	16%	17%
Employees	370	378	330	360	430

The astonishing improvements in 1996 to 1997 are made possible by Tom Baron's simplification of business processes, products and services to enable BTG to become the 'best cost' (for equivalent quality) in a narrower range of market. Although never having read Porter or about Jack Welch's simplification programmes at General Electric, Tom Baron appears to understand intuitively what the 'management gurus' have discovered and embellished intellectually.

Final questions to the reader

1. How plausible do you believe each individual Scenario is?
2. What other key scenario(s) do you believe we have missed? (Consider major change factors which could either help success or generate failure.)
3. Given the range of possible futures why do you believe that management more generally tend to have a single 'mind-set' on future strategic change (which switches from being either 'optimistic' to 'pessimistic')?
4. Under Scenario 1 ('competitive success') what problems do you foresee in what BTG 'does for an encore' — given that it has the management team from an earlier stage of its evolution?
5. Under Scenario 2 ('continued decline'), do you believe that in 1993 you should have yourself orchestrated a boardroom coup to remove Sam Wheeze or perhaps floated the idea of a merger with a friendly but more powerful partner?
6. Under Scenario 3 ('nose dive and turnaround') do you think that given the complexity and interdependency of BTG's activities this turnaround in financial results is plausible? Could Tom Baron's actions (especially in reducing numbers) have put BTG into a faster downward spiral through losing key staff?

CONCLUSIONS AND LESSONS FROM BLACKBRIDGE TECHNOLOGY

This case simulation gives some insight into the process of change of an organisation over a 15-year timespan. This highlights how an organisation with strength and vision can lose its way and go for considerable periods of time without even realising that this has occurred.

It should also make clear the importance of managing strategy, structure and culture coherently, as well as the perils of opting for incremental change when a more fundamental shift is required. The role of leadership was also emphasised, as well as that of understanding 'the paradigm' (particularly in managing acquisitions and becoming international). The benefits and dangers of strategic intent or 'mission' were also well illustrated. Lastly, the performance data highlighted lags between strategic health (and illness) and financial performance.

Suggested issues arising from stimulus questions:

Question 1

Key challenges for the newly combined group might include:

- culture clash following 'integration';
- management structure and power sharing;
- retaining middle management (especially in Megathink);
- site location;
- synergies between both companies, especially knowledge sharing;
- management processes — especially the strategic and financial planning and control;
- coping with a backlog of problems from (undigested) past growth;
- competitive threat to Blackbridge;
- revitalising Megathink.

Question 2

Comments on Sam Wheeze's priorities for managing strategic change:

- Culture is likely to provide more of a blockage in the longer-term than perhaps structure.
- The 'structure' which has emerged feels like a 'compromise' effort. Also, it may not be such a good idea to exclude Mary Morbid from the group board considering the extensive people-related issues which are at the core of the strategic change problem.
- There is an apparent major gap in not devising a more fleshed-out strategy, particularly in view of the increasing complexity of strategic choices which the new board will face.

Question 3

On your options for timing an intervention in the away day:

- Unless you intervene immediately your silence will be taken as tacit approval.
- If you raise questions in a mild way these are very likely to be dismissed by Sam Wheeze.
- This appears to suggest a relatively direct and forceful probing of thinking — this will need, however, to be calmly conducted so as not to be exposing yourself to being 'thrown overboard' at the earliest opportunity.

Question 4

On Blackbridge's strategic intent:

- The argument about the 'growth rate' is an excellent example of *how not* to formulate a strategy: although it raises important issues about sustainability and capability, it belies a whole range of assumptions about market and competitive change and about competitive position across each of the market places which Blackbridge is in or is seeking to enter.
- The premise that 'growth is good' warrants closer analysis: growth can destroy as well as create shareholder value as margins may be eroded, the organisation becomes overstretched and overcomplex and where investment is absorbed to support competitive strategies offering minimal returns.

Question 5

Securing the facilitator:

- Malcolm Magic has shown himself to be a valuable change agent with whom you can share the intervention role: it looks as if you *must* persuade Sam Wheeze to lock Malcolm Magic into the process.
- If cost is a major concern can Malcolm be persuaded to pre-book some 'core days' to meet with the team so that Blackbridge's committed cost is lower but you have Malcolm Magic tied in.

Question 6

Driving the point home:

- Malcolm Magic has indeed done a good job but, on his own, he is in danger of being an 'island' of concern with the strategy which might easily be shrugged off.
- It may, therefore, be opportune to suggest a 'way out' — particularly to work bottom-upwards to arrive at a 'feasible strategy' rather than to persist in a strategic intent (or more properly 'ambition') which is only likely to result in the phenomenon of 'strategic droop' — of plans never fully met.

Question 7

Sam Wheeze digs in:

- It does seem as though Sam Wheeze's mind appears to close down very quickly despite sound advice from several sources.
- This raises the real concern that Sam Wheeze does not have the calibre (as manager or as leader) to take Blackbridge through another phase of successful development.

Final questions to the reader

These questions highlight the multiple factors which face all organisations operating in a turbulent environment. Whilst some factors are less controllable, many more are controllable — either in whole or in part. Even where factors are less controllable, the way in which an organisation positions itself — in its external markets, in its style of competing, in how it allocates resources and most importantly of all in its mind-set — all these factors can be controlled to some degree.

Scenario 1 ('competitive success') looks optimistic and less plausible. Scenario 2 ('continued decline') appears far more plausible and there is a severe risk that Scenario 3 ('nose dive and turnaround') could occur on present trends. There may be other scenarios too, such as being taken over or going out of business.

In the less pleasant scenarios, the reality is likely to unfold suddenly. Companies often struggle along for some time beyond the point at which disease becomes terminal. Managers are adept at making things appear 'normal' well beyond the point where turnaround has become urgent, as has been witnessed by the demise of many 1980s stock market 'stars' in the UK in the early 1990s.

Lastly, on the topic of 'what actually happened', we will have to say 'watch this space'. But BTG will certainly face a steep uphill climb just to survive. Past successes have numbed the organisation to the possibility of failure — so a critical success factor will be a strong dose of strategic realism.

REFERENCES

Anderson, E S, Grunde, K V, Haug, T and Turner, J R (1987) *Goal Directed Project Management*, Kogan Page, London

Ansoff, I (1982) Understanding and Managing Strategic Change, North Holland (Elsevier), Amsterdam

Argyris, C (1977) *Double Loop Learning in Organisations*, Harvard Business Review, pp 115-125, September-October

Argyris, C (1991) *Teaching Smart People How to Learn*, Harvard Business Review, pp 99-109, May-June

Beer, M, Eisenstaat, R A, Spector, B (1990) *The Critical Path to Corporate Renewal*, Harvard Business School Press

Boogan, M G and Komocar, J M (1990) 'Directing Strategic Change: A dynamic Holistic Approach', pp 135-165, *Mapping Strategic Thought*, Huff A S, J Wiley & Sons, Chichester

Bowman, C (1992) 'Interpreting Competitive Strategy' and 'Charting Competitive Strategy' in *The Challenge of Strategic Management*, Faulkner, D and Johnson, G, Kogan Page, London

Campbell, A and Tawadey, K (1990) *Mission and Business Philosophy – Winning Employee Commitment*, Heinemann Publishing, Oxford

Carnall, C A (1986) 'Managing Strategic Change: An Integrated Approach', *Long Range Planning*, vol 19, December, pp 105-115

Carnal, C A (1990) *Managing Change*, Routledge, London

Garratt, B (1990) *Creating a Learning Organisation*, Director Books, Cambridge

Ghemawat, P (1991) *Commitment — the Dynamic of Strategy*, Macmillan, New York

Gleick, J (1990) *Chaos*, Penguin, London

Gluck, F et al (1982) 'The four phases of strategic management', *Journal of Business Strategy*, 2 (3), 9-21

Goold, M and Quinn, J (1990) *Strategic Control*, Economist Books, London

Grundy, A and King, D (1992) 'Using Strategic Planning to Drive Strategic Change', *Long Range Planning*, vol 25 no 1, February, pp 100-108

Grundy, A N (1992) *Corporate Strategy and Financial Decisions*, Kogan Page, London

Handy, C (1989) *The Age of Unreason*, Business Books, London

Johnson, G (1988) *Exploring Corporate Strategy*, Prentice-Hall, Hemel Hempstead

Johnson, G (1992) 'Managing Strategic Change — Structure, Culture and Action', *Long Range Planning*, vol 25 no 1, February, pp 22-36

Kanter, R M (1983) *The Change Masters*, Unwin, London

Kanter, R M (1989) *When Giants Learn to Dance*, Simon and Schuster, Hemel Hempstead

Kuhn, T S (1962) *The Structure of Scientific Revolutions*, Chicago University Press, Chicago

Lewin, K (1935) *A Dynamic Theory of Personality*, McGraw Book Company, New York

Mintzberg, H (1978) *Patterns in Strategy Formation*, Management Science, pp 934-48, May

Pascale, R T (1990) *Managing on the Edge*, Penguin, London

Peters, T (1987) *Thriving on Chaos*, Macmillan, London

Peters, T and Waterman, R H (1982) *In Search of Excellence*, Harper & Row, New York

Pettigrew, A and Whipp, R (1991) *Managing Change for Competitive Success*, Basil Blackwell, Oxford

REFERENCES

Piercy, N (1989) 'Diagnosing and solving implementation problems in strategic planning', *Journal of General Management*, vol 15, no 1, Autumn

Porter, E M (1985) *Competitive Advantage*, The Free Press, New York

Quinn, J B (1980) *Strategy for Change — Logical Incrementalism*, Richard D Irwin, Illinois

Schaffer, R H and Thomson, H A (1992) *Successful Change Programs Begin With Results*, Harvard Business Review, January-February

Senge, P M (1990) *The Fifth Discipline: The Art and Practice of the Learning Organisation*, Century Business, London

Stonich, P (1982) *Implementing Strategy — Making Strategy Happen*, Ballinger, New York

Ulrich, D and Lake, D (1990) *Organisational Capability*, J Wiley & Sons, New York

Welch, J (1989) Interview with Tichy, N and Charan, R, *Speed, Simplicity and Self-Confidence*, Harvard Business Review, pp 112-120, September-October

INDEX